AF688782

Marketing2aT

Become the Marketer Every Team Wants

GROUNDED IN 130+ INTERVIEWS,
CURRENT RESEARCH, AND
40 PRACTICAL MOVES
WITH AI-GUIDED PROMPTS.

David LaCombe

Marketing2aT: Become the Marketer Every Team Wants

Copyright © 2026 by David LaCombe

All rights reserved. No part of this book may be reproduced, stored in a retrieval system, or transmitted in any form or by any means—electronic, mechanical, photocopying, recording, or otherwise—without prior written permission from the publisher, except for brief quotations used in reviews or critical articles.

Published by OrangeCo Press

[New Windsor, NY]

ISBN: 979-8-99319-061-7 (paperback)
ISBN: 979-8-99319-062-4 (ebook)

Library of Congress Control Number: 2026911687

Names: LaCombe, David, author.
Title: Marketing2aT: become the marketer every team wants / David LaCombe.
Description: First edition. | New Windsor, NY : OrangeCo Press, [2026] | Audience: college students. | Includes bibliographical references and index.
Identifiers: LCCN: 2026911687 | ISBN: 9798993190617 (paperback) | 9798993190624 (ebook)
Subjects: LCSH: Marketing. | Marketing--Vocational guidance. | Career development. | Success in business. | Business communication. | Creative ability in business. | Strategic planning. | Teams in the workplace. | LCGFT: Instructional and educational works. | Handbooks and manuals. | BISAC: BUSINESS & ECONOMICS / Marketing / General. | BUSINESS & ECONOMICS / Careers / General. | BUSINESS & ECONOMICS / Skills.
Classification: LCC: HF5415.1 .L33 2026 | DDC: 658.8--dc23

First edition
Printed in the United States of America

For KC, my wife, my sounding board, and my favorite person to get lost in thought with. Some of our best ideas began during windshield time. So did this book.

Get the tools behind the book

I created a free reader toolkit to help you use what you learn here.

Scan for a short welcome video from the author, the discussion guide, Ask AI for Help prompts, and resources designed to help you build skills employers value.

FREE READER TOOLKIT

TABLE OF CONTENTS

INTRODUCTION

You're not sure you're ready.

Maybe you're finishing a marketing degree and realizing the gap between what you learned in class and what employers expect is wider than anyone warned you. Or maybe you're in your first or second role, working hard and hitting your numbers, but sensing something is missing—some invisible curriculum everyone else seems to have completed.

Maybe you're pivoting into marketing from another field, bringing skills you know are valuable but struggling to translate them into a language hiring managers will understand.

Whatever brought you here, you've probably had the same quiet thought: *I should be further along by now.*

You read job descriptions that require five years of experience for entry-level positions. You sit in meetings where people toss around acronyms you've never heard before. You watch colleagues receive promotions and wonder what they know that you don't. The imposter in your mind has a lot to say, and most of it isn't kind.

Here's what I want you to understand: those feelings do not mean you're failing. They mean you're paying attention. And what you're sensing is real — not a confidence problem, not a perception problem, but an actual gap between what the profession demands and what most marketers, at every level, actually know. A 2026 Ipsos study tested 1,226 practicing marketers on foundational marketing concepts across four countries. Only 35 percent cleared the bar. Two in three working professionals, people already in the roles you're trying to reach, could not demonstrate basic mastery of the field they're paid to practice.

You are not behind. You are just honest about it. That's rarer than you think, and it's the better starting point.

Why Early-Career Marketers Need This Book

Marketing2aT is designed to help you become the type of marketer employers trust with tougher challenges, broader responsibilities, and faster-paced changes. It won't provide shortcuts or hollow confidence. Instead, it will help you develop the judgment, habits, and cross-functional fluency that distinguish marketers who continue to grow from those who get stuck.

If the job market feels tougher than you expected, you're not imagining it. But the reason might not be what you think.

The common explanations—too many graduates, not enough entry-level jobs, and AI replacing people—are only partly true. But those are just symptoms; the real change is structural.

Why Marketing Careers Feel Different Now

Starting in 2023 and accelerating through 2025 and 2026, the world's largest technology companies began investing huge amounts of capital into artificial intelligence infrastructure: data centers, chips, networking, and power supplies. That decision did more than boost the development of new tools. It changed expectations throughout the business world.

This is more than just a technology story. It's about how capital gets allocated, and that distinction matters.

When the world's largest companies redirect their capital on such a scale, the impact doesn't stay confined. Boards that once tolerated vague marketing budgets now ask more precise questions. CFOs who once accepted "directionally right" campaign results now require revenue impact, margin contribution, and cash timing. Hiring managers revise job descriptions—not because a memo instructed them to, but because the company's economic logic has shifted beneath them.

The result is a labor market doing two things at once. It is shrinking in areas where you were trained to handle—content creation, basic audience segmentation, templated email campaigns, and routine social media management. AI manages these tasks faster, cheaper, and at a scale no junior employee can match.

At the same time, the market is growing in areas where most programs haven't prepared you: AI marketing operations. Revenue analytics. Prompt-driven demand generation. Roles that sit at the crossroads of marketing strategy and technical skills. Positions that require you to understand not just what happened in a campaign, but why it happened and whether the investment was effective.

The scale of this restructuring is not speculative. A 2025 study by the Burning Glass Institute and Harvard Business School's Project on Managing the Future of Work found that generative AI could automate nearly 18 million entry-level jobs in the United States—about 12 percent of the total workforce—including roles in marketing, legal support, and project management (Fuller et al., 2025).

However, the same research revealed a surprising finding: about 29 million higher-level "mastery roles" could become available to a larger pool of candidates as AI lowers technical barriers to entry. These jobs aren't simply disappearing. They're shifting from routine tasks to roles that require judgment, adaptability, and the ability to oversee systems you didn't create. The question for early-career marketers is not whether this shift is happening; it's whether you'll be on the side of growth or the side of decline.

So when someone tells you the job market is tough, that's true. But "tough" doesn't fully capture it. The market isn't hostile; it's reorganizing. The money didn't disappear from marketing; it shifted to a different kind of marketing. And the companies doing the hiring are looking for a different type of marketer. That's the gap this book aims to close.

The Book I Wished I Had Earlier

For the record, I never planned to become a marketer.

For my first two decades of work, I served as a paramedic, responding to calls in the middle of the night, making quick assessments under pressure, and learning to stay calm amid chaos. It shaped how I think. But eventually, I wanted a different life. So I shifted into business with no plan or connections, armed with a skill set that didn't fit easily into a résumé.

My first role was in product management. Then I moved into marketing, then sales, then customer experience, and finally strategic relationship management. Each transition felt like starting over, with unexpected learning curves and unwritten rules no one had explained. I spent more time than I'd like to admit feeling uncertain: unsure what success looked like, unsure whether I was measuring up, and unsure whom to ask for help without seeming like I didn't belong. Sound familiar?

Some of my transitions went smoothly. I found mentors who supported me, uncovered strengths I hadn't known I had, and shifted from operations to leadership, eventually becoming a CMO.

But I also stumbled—more than once. I was overly confident in situations that required careful listening. I made relationship choices I would later regret, like burning bridges I should have kept and ignoring connections that could have opened doors. I confused activity with real progress. I learned most lessons the hard way because I was too stubborn to accept them any other way. I'm telling you this because it's true and because it's why I wrote this book.

The leaders I respect most aren't the ones who always get everything right. They're the ones who make enough mistakes to develop judgment and get enough things right to stay in the game long enough to apply that wisdom.

I've been a business leader for over twenty years, and I'm still learning. The 130-plus interviews I conducted for this book taught me things I wish I'd understood decades earlier—patterns I'd sensed but couldn't name, common mistakes, and principles that could have saved me years of trial and error.

If I'd had this book when I was transitioning out of emergency medicine, I would have made fewer mistakes and understood the ones I did make better. That's what I want for you.

Throughout my journey, I observed that successful marketers weren't always the most technically skilled or the most highly credentialed. Instead, they were the ones who knew how to learn, think across boundaries, and connect their work to meaningful business issues. They were, in a word, T-shaped.

The T-Shaped Marketer, Explained

The T-shaped professional possesses deep expertise in one or more areas—the vertical stroke—combined with broad fluency across related disciplines—the horizontal stroke. I wanted a book that explains how to become T-shaped. Not tactics. Not certification prep. I wanted a book that covers the developmental work—thinking, habits, and character—that separates marketers who get stuck from those who keep growing.

That book didn't exist, so I wrote it.

Over more than two years, I interviewed over 130 C-suite executives, founders, specialists, and consultants. I started each interview with one question: *"Tell me about a time when a marketer either delighted you or failed to meet your expectations."*

The patterns were clear: Technical skills are important, but they're just the beginning. What set apart the marketers who advanced from those who stayed stuck was a group of abilities rarely seen on résumés: continuous learning, critical thinking, cross-functional communication, managing ambiguity, taking ownership of results, and growing without being told to.

I organized these into a framework called T-GROWTH, with each chapter exploring one dimension through insights from practitioners who have applied these capabilities.

Let me be direct about the stakes.

Marketing advances faster than academic programs adapt. Tasks that were entry-level five years ago—like content creation, campaign templates, and simple analytics—are now managed by AI tools funded by the same investment cycle that's transforming the industry. These tools become cheaper and more powerful each quarter. If your only competitive advantage is doing tasks that software can copy, you're in a race you can't win.

The market isn't just eliminating roles; it's creating new ones. These positions demand the ability to connect marketing efforts to revenue, margins, and cash flow. These roles aren't determined by whether you can operate AI-powered platforms because soon everyone will be able to do that. The real distinction is whether you can recognize when the AI makes mistakes, whether you can identify patterns from causes, or differentiate a correlation from a decision worth funding.

Employers are frustrated with candidates who have credentials but lack critical thinking or ownership. They're not demanding perfection; they want judgment—the ability that comes from understanding how a business actually functions, not just how a campaign performs.

If you develop only narrow technical skills, you'll be competing against software that gets cheaper each year. If you focus solely on broad generalist knowledge, you'll lack the depth needed to be truly useful. Successful marketers possess both—they are credible enough to be trusted and versatile enough to handle different tasks.

That's what being a T-shaped marketer means. In a market where every marketing dollar faces greater scrutiny, T-shaped isn't just aspirational. It's the minimum.

This is a practitioner's book. Although I teach graduate marketing students at a private university in NYC, the core of this book comes from real work, real leaders, and real consequences. The voices here are practitioners, too. When a marketing consultant talks about building a career without a degree, she speaks from experience. When a vice president of strategy describes volunteering for the toughest jobs on an aircraft carrier, he explains how he learned to learn. I've woven their stories into frameworks and reflection questions, but the core wisdom comes from people who've walked the path you're on now.

If you're a manager, this is the book you give to someone you believe in, saying, "I want you to read this because I believe in you."

How to Use This Book

Each chapter follows a consistent structure that guides you from insight to action. You'll meet characters in situations you'll recognize. Anthony, Nala, and Mia are fictional—but nothing about them is invented. They are composites based on patterns that emerged across more than 130 interviews with executives, hiring managers, and marketers at different points in their careers.

Their struggles, doubts, and decisions reflect real moments I've heard described in various rooms by different people, using very similar language. They have been boiled down into characters so you can grasp the lesson before it's explained.

Anthony is a marketing student in his early twenties, navigating his first serious internship. He understands the language of campaigns and social metrics. What he is still learning is how businesses actually generate profit.

Nala is a few years ahead, working as a brand manager; she's capable and respected, quietly questioning whether credibility is earned by fitting in or by standing for something.

Mia is even more capable. She's a product marketer with strong analytical skills and sharp strategic thinking. Her challenge is to learn how to ensure that her thinking influences those who make decisions. You may see parts of yourself in one of them, or in all three.

You'll also hear directly from the leaders I interviewed, including their advice, warnings, and hard-won insights into what separates marketers who grow from those who get stuck. These are not polished sound bites; these are the voices of practitioners who remember what it felt like to be in your shoes now.

You will also discover practical tools called MOVEs—specific actions you can take right away to develop each skill. In street slang, "making moves" means taking deliberate action to improve your situation, hustling with purpose. That's exactly what these sections offer: small experiments you can try, skills you can develop, and habits you can build.

Each MOVE includes an AI prompt to help you explore the concept deeply. These prompts aren't shortcuts; they're thinking partners. They teach you to use AI as a development tool, not a replacement. When used effectively, they speed up your learning. When used lazily, they teach you nothing. The choice is yours.

What This Book Is, and Isn't

I want to be upfront about limits. This book won't turn you into an expert overnight. Gaining expertise takes years of intentional practice, and no book can shorten that process. What this book does is show you what to practice and why it matters.

This book doesn't guarantee you'll get a job. The market is competitive, timing matters, and luck plays a role that no one wants to admit.

What this book can do is help you become the kind of candidate employers remember and call back.

This book will not replace the hard work of building relationships, shipping projects, and learning from failure. There are no hacks, secrets, or tricks here. What this book can do is help you understand what the work actually is, so you stop wasting effort on things that don't compound.

So, here's my invitation. Read with a pen in hand. Mark what resonates. Engage with the MOVE stories and related AI prompts. Treat this not as content to consume but as a conversation to continue. What resonates now may feel different a year from now. That's intentional. This is a book you grow into, not one you outgrow.

You don't need to have everything figured out. The leaders in this book didn't, and most would say they still don't. What they developed, and what you can too, is a willingness to keep learning, the humility to admit what you don't know, and the discipline to close the important gaps.

This book won't turn you into an expert overnight, but it will help you become the kind of marketer that leaders trust with tough problems. That's what being a T-shaped marketer means, and that's what I hope this book helps you achieve.

Welcome to *Marketing2aT*.

Works Cited

Fuller, J., Sigelman, M., & Fenlon, M. (2025, March 10). How Gen AI could change the value of expertise. Harvard Business Review.

Ipsos. (2026). Marketing anchors: The case for capability in an era of transformation.

CHAPTER 1: THE SHAPE OF A MARKETING CAREER

"The illiterate of the 21st century will not be those who cannot read and write, but those who cannot learn, unlearn, and relearn."
—Alvin Toffler

You did what you were supposed to do.

You studied the frameworks. You learned the platforms. You built the portfolio. You collected the credentials meant to open doors. Now you're looking at a job market that seems to want something different from what you were trained to provide.

You already know why. The introduction to this book outlined the capital reallocation reshaping the marketing industry: hundreds of billions flowing into AI infrastructure, the increased scrutiny of marketing budgets, and the simultaneous shrinking of traditional roles and growth of new ones. That's the landscape. This chapter explains how to navigate it.

Because the question isn't whether the market has changed, but what employers actually want from the marketers they still hire. The answer, it turns out, is different from what most people expect.

What Employers Actually Want

For this book, I interviewed over 130 executives, founders, and hiring managers. I asked them a straightforward question: Tell me about a time when a marketer either impressed you or failed to meet your expectations.

The answers surprised me, not because they were unusual but because they were so consistent and so different from what most career advice assumes.

I expected to hear about technical skills. I expected leaders to complain about marketers who couldn't run attribution models, optimize paid campaigns, or build automation workflows. Those complaints came up occasionally, but they weren't what kept leaders awake at night.

Three findings stood out.

First: Employers value good judgment in complex situations more than early technical expertise. The marketers who impressed leaders weren't the ones who arrived knowing every tool. They were the ones who could handle ambiguity, ask insightful questions, and make reasonable decisions despite incomplete information. Technical skills mattered, but those skills were basic requirements, not standout qualities. One CMO told me she would rather hire someone who admits uncertainty and thinks clearly than someone who projects confidence yet misses the point.

This finding is more significant in the current capital environment. When every marketing dollar competes with AI infrastructure investment for budget approval, the cost of poor judgment increases. A misallocated campaign budget isn't just a missed opportunity; it's money the CFO might argue should have been spent elsewhere altogether. The leaders I interviewed expressed a preference. They described a survival necessity.

Second: Reliable follow-through earns more trust than bold ideas that never come to fruition. Leaders recounted numerous stories about marketers who proposed campaigns and concepts but failed to deliver. Those who succeeded were often less flashy but reliable. They took ownership of outcomes and closed loops, consistently fulfilling commitments without oversight. "I'll take boring and reliable over brilliant and flaky every time," one VP of Marketing told me. "Brilliant and reliable is ideal, but if I have to choose, reliability wins."

The economic environment amplifies this. Boards and CFOs no longer fund promising ideas based on potential alone. Budgets are harder to justify, approval cycles are longer, and leaders who stake their credibility on a project need to be confident it will actually be delivered. Execution has become the main measure of trust because the economic climate no longer tolerates waste.

Third: Business empathy across functions is more important than overly confident marketing answers. Marketers who struggled often spoke only in marketing jargon—impressions, engagement, brand awareness—without connecting their efforts to revenue, profit, or customer lifetime value. Those who succeeded could sit in a room with finance, sales, and product teams and translate their work into terms that mattered to each function. They understood that marketing does not exist in isolation but to support business results.

In a high-pressure environment where the CFO's questions become tougher and the board's patience shortens, this skill has shifted from being a nice extra to a basic requirement. Successful marketers today understand what finance is protecting, what sales is promising, and what operations are limited by. Cross-functional empathy isn't just a soft skill; it's how you gain access to the rooms where budgets are decided. None of this appears on a typical marketing syllabus. And that's exactly the problem.

The T-Shaped Advantage

There's a model that captures what these employers seek. It's called the T-shaped professional.

The idea of "T-shaped" professionals originates from the 1980s and was popularized by Tim Brown, then CEO of the innovation firm IDEO, as the model he used to build teams.

The term stuck because it describes something real. Imagine the letter T. The vertical line stands for depth, representing specialized expertise in a specific area. For marketers, this could be demand generation, content strategy, product marketing, analytics, or branding. It's the skill you excel at more than most people in the room, the ability that makes you valuable from day one.

The horizontal stroke signifies breadth, your capacity to collaborate across disciplines, speak multiple professional languages, and connect your expertise to the larger picture. It's what makes you more than just a specialist. It's what makes you valuable in various functions.

A word of caution: skill acquisition is a continuous process, not a one-time event. Researchers Stuart Dreyfus and Hubert Dreyfus initially outlined how professionals advance through stages of skill acquisition, from novice to advanced beginner, competent, proficient, and ultimately expert. Patricia Benner later adapted this model to nursing, demonstrating that practitioners develop intuitive judgment through deliberate practice rather than just by gaining years of experience. The same idea holds true in marketing.

Here's what this means for you: Your skills are adaptable to different situations. You might be skilled in content strategy but still a novice in marketing analytics. You could have expert judgment in brand positioning but be an advanced beginner in paid media. This is normal. The vertical stroke of the T is not just a straight line; it's a profile with peaks and valleys that change as you develop.

What moves you along the continuum is not time in a role. It is deliberate practice, the focused, feedback-rich repetition that builds genuine capability. Ten years of repeating the same tasks teaches you far less than two years spent stretching into uncomfortable territory, reflecting on what worked, and adjusting your approach.

The horizontal stroke represents breadth—fluency across adjacent disciplines. It's understanding how sales works, how finance measures success, how product teams prioritize, and how customers make decisions. It's the ability to collaborate across boundaries, translate across functions, and see how your work connects to the larger business.

Most early-career marketers have been trained to build the vertical stroke. They have studied campaign management, learned to use analytics platforms, and practiced content creation. That foundation matters. Without depth, you have nothing to offer. Depth alone isn't enough anymore.

Develop only narrow technical skills, and you'll compete against software that keeps getting cheaper each year. AI can already write copy, analyze data, segment audiences, and optimize campaigns. What it cannot do, at least not yet, is understand organizational politics, build trust with skeptical stakeholders, or exercise judgment when data is incomplete and the stakes are high.

Develop only broad generalist knowledge, and you'll lack the credibility to be trusted with real problems. Breadth without depth is dilettantism.

You need to be genuinely good at something before anyone will listen to your perspective on anything else.

The marketers who thrive are the ones who build both: deep enough to be useful, wide enough to be versatile. That's the T-shaped advantage. And it's what this book will help you develop.

Why Technical Skills Aren't Enough

The interviews confirm what the research already indicates. Reviewing marketing job postings reveals that employers look for learning agility and cross-functional collaboration nearly as much as specific technical skills. Surveys also show that hiring managers consistently prioritize curiosity, adaptability, and communication over platform proficiency when assessing early-career candidates.

In a large workforce study, 77 percent of graduates reported learning more in their first six months on the job than during their entire degree program, and 93 percent of HR leaders identified curiosity and a willingness to learn as essential mindsets for new hires (Hult International Business School & Workplace Intelligence, 2025).

The market is sending you a message. Technical skills open the door. Everything else decides if you stay and move forward.

Industry groups have created competency frameworks that define the technical and strategic capabilities marketers need. The American Marketing Association's Professional Certified Marketer domains, the Chartered Institute of Marketing's professional standards, and similar resources provide clear views of the profession's expectations. These frameworks are valuable to review. They offer common language, specific benchmarks, and practical development pathways.

What this book adds is the developmental layer beneath those frameworks: the habits of mind, character, and judgment that determine whether technical skills lead to career advancement. Competency frameworks tell you what to learn. T-GROWTH guides you on how to learn it and how to integrate what you've learned into a cohesive professional identity.

Technical skills matter—immensely. You must be competent in a specific area before anyone will trust you with broader responsibility. The vertical stroke comes first. If you stop there, you'll plateau sooner than you expect.

The horizontal stroke—the breadth—is what builds over time. It's what moves you from being a task-doer to a problem-solver, from a specialist to a strategic partner, and from someone who simply executes campaigns to someone who shapes them.

Connect Marketing Work to Business Outcomes

Every generation of marketers has had to adapt. This one has to adapt faster, to bigger forces, with less margin for error than any that came before.

The introduction to this book described a historic capital reallocation cycle in which the largest technology companies are redirecting nearly all of their free cash flow into AI infrastructure. This investment sets new expectations for every downstream company.

Boards that once reviewed marketing budgets annually now do so quarterly. CFOs who previously accepted "the campaign performed well" now question if the spending was the best way to use that capital compared to other options. Hiring managers who used to look for potential now require proof that a candidate can connect their work to measurable business results.

That pressure has uncovered something the profession usually avoids discussing. The knowledge gaps most likely to harm you in that environment aren't in emerging tools or AI fluency. They're in the core concepts that answer the CFO's most basic question: why this investment, and why now?

In a study of over 1,200 practicing marketers across four countries, the weakest areas weren't platform skills or tactical execution. They were concepts such as excess share of voice, media neutrality, and penetration, which are core elements of investment logic (Ipsos, 2026). A marketer who can't define ESOV can't defend a budget using it. Foundational knowledge isn't just academic; it's the language of professional credibility.

This is the environment for which the T-GROWTH framework was designed. The framework was developed through discussions with executives, hiring managers, and marketing leaders who make decisions in this economic setting. Their responses reflect the pressures they face today, not those from five years ago. When they describe what they look for, they are expressing what this specific economic moment requires.

T-GROWTH isn't about following trends or collecting certifications. It's about developing core skills that stay valuable regardless of which platforms succeed or fail. Curiosity. Integrity. Empathy. Communication. Strategic thinking. Adaptability. Integration. These skills don't become outdated. They form the foundation that enables you to learn whatever comes next.

The marketers who will succeed in the next decade are those who have not only mastered today's tools but also developed the judgment to handle whatever tools come next.

The T-GROWTH Framework for Career Growth

After analyzing over 130 interviews and desk research on employer expectations, I identified seven key skills that separate marketers who succeed from those who stall. I have organized these skills into a framework called T-GROWTH.

These are competencies that emerged organically from conversations with people who hire, manage, and develop marketers. When I asked what separated the best from the rest, these seven themes kept recurring.

	Dimension	Description
T	**Thirst to Learn**	The foundation of everything else. Curiosity, teachability, and the humility to admit what you don't know. Without it, every other capability stagnates.
G	**Grit and Integrity**	Resilience under pressure, ownership of outcomes, and the ethical backbone to do the right thing when no one is watching. These qualities build trust.
R	**Relate and Empathize**	Emotional intelligence, active listening, and the ability to build authentic relationships across functions. Marketing is a team sport. This is how you play it.
O	**Observe and Communicate**	Superior writing, clear thinking, and the ability to translate data into insight. The skill that separates marketers who influence decisions from those who merely report on them.

W	**Wisdom Before Strategy**	Critical thinking, business acumen, and the ability to connect marketing activities to financial outcomes. This is how you earn a seat at the table.
T	**Tech Fluency and Adaptability**	Comfort with new tools, a willingness to experiment, and the versatility to pivot as the landscape shifts. In a field transformed by AI, this is survival.
H	**Holistic Growth**	The integration of all of the above into a coherent professional identity. Not just accumulating skills but developing the judgment to know when and how to apply them.

Each letter in T-GROWTH represents a chapter in this book. Every chapter examines one aspect through the perspectives of practitioners who have experienced it—executives who hire marketers, leaders who develop them, and professionals who have navigated the same transitions you are facing.

Why Each Dimension Matters Now

You might interpret that table as a list of desirable qualities. It isn't. Each dimension corresponds to a specific demand imposed by the capital environment you are entering.

Thirst to Learn matters because tools are evolving faster than any curriculum can keep up—supported by hundreds of billions in infrastructure spending that ensures continued progress. Graduates who stop learning after graduation will be obsolete before their first promotion.

Grit and Integrity matter because tighter budgets and increased scrutiny create environments with more pressure, greater ambiguity, and less margin for error. Resilience is a professional requirement when the economic environment does not forgive easily.

Relate and Empathize matters because cross-functional collaboration is key when capital allocation decisions involve marketing, finance, sales, and operations at the same table. You can't influence people you don't understand.

Observe and Communicate matters because the signal-to-noise ratio in AI-generated data is deteriorating, not improving. More tools producing more output lead to increased chances of mistaking correlation for causation. The ability to see clearly and communicate precisely becomes more valuable when clarity is limited.

Wisdom Before Strategy matters because "where does this show up in revenue, margin, and cash?" is now the baseline question, not the advanced one. Financial empathy, understanding what the people who control budgets care about and why, is the skill that separates marketers who present dashboards from marketers who inform decisions.

Tech Fluency and Adaptability matters because AI fluency is rapidly becoming table stakes. Within two years, employers will assume you can operate AI-powered platforms. The differentiator won't be whether you can use the tools. It will be whether you can tell when the tools are wrong.

Holistic Growth matters because careers built in volatile capital environments rarely follow linear paths. The professionals who sustain performance over decades are the ones who invest in their whole selves—not just their technical skills—because the market will ask them to adapt in ways they can't currently predict.

None of this is theoretical. Every dimension in this framework was validated by people who are hiring, managing, and promoting marketers right now, in the middle of the largest capital reallocation cycle in a generation.

The framework prepares you for a present that most marketing programs haven't caught up to yet. That's the head start. Use it.

Your Move

You picked up this book because something doesn't add up. The credentials you earned don't feel like enough. The job market seems to want something you weren't taught. The path forward isn't as clear as you were promised.

That uncertainty is valid. The gap is real. So is the opportunity. The employers I spoke with aren't searching for perfection. They're seeking growth in people who learn quickly, take ownership of their development, and arrive prepared to expand. They're after the capabilities this book teaches. They're looking for T-shaped marketers.

You don't need to have everything figured out. However, you do need to know what to focus on and how to approach it. That's what T-GROWTH offers: a guide for the developmental work that separates marketers who get stuck from those who keep growing.

Read with intention. Engage the MOVEs. Use the AI prompts not as answers but as starting points. Treat this book as an ongoing conversation, not just content to consume.

The gap between your current position and your goal needs to be bridged. Let's begin crossing that bridge together.

Works Cited

American Marketing Association. (n.d.). Professional Certified Marketer (PCM) certifications and domains. American Marketing Association.

Benner, P. (2004). Using the Dreyfus model of skill acquisition to describe and interpret skill acquisition and clinical judgment in nursing practice and education. Bulletin of Science, Technology & Society, 24(3), 188-199.

Brown, T. (2009, September). On being T-shaped. Core77.

Chartered Institute of Marketing. (n.d.). Global Professional Marketing Framework. The Chartered Institute of Marketing.

Dreyfus, H. L., & Dreyfus, S. E. (1986). Mind over machine: The power of human intuition and expertise in the era of the computer. Free Press.

Hult International Business School & Workplace Intelligence. (2025). College graduate skills study: Recent graduates and HR leaders on education and workplace readiness. Hult International Business School.

Ipsos. (2026). Marketing anchors: The case for capability in an era of transformation.

CHAPTER 2: THIRST TO LEARN

"In times of change, learners inherit the earth,
while the learned find themselves beautifully equipped to
deal with a world that no longer exists."
—Eric Hoffer

Field Story: The Second Interview

Anthony thought the interview was over.

He had met the VP of Marketing, reviewed his portfolio, and answered the standard questions about his strengths and weaknesses. As he closed his notebook, the VP smiled and said, "Our director of finance wants to meet you, too. He's free in ten minutes. Up for another round?"

His stomach flipped. Finance was his weakest subject. *You're not analytical enough,* an inside voice whispered. *Real marketers have already figured this out.*

Ten minutes later, Anthony sat across from the finance leader in a small conference room. No slides. No laptop. Just a legal pad and a pen.

He started simply, "Tell me, in plain language, how this company makes money."

Anthony hesitated. He knew the product's features, the audience, and even the brand's social channels. But the revenue model? Margins? How is marketing tied to profit?

Nope. You should've known this. You're going to blow it.

He took a breath. "Honestly," he said, "I can't explain that well yet. I read your annual report, but I focused more on the brand story than on the numbers. I should've dug deeper."

The finance director nodded kindly. "Appreciate the honesty. So, what would you do in your first thirty days here to close that gap?"

This time, he had more to say.

"I'd start by listening. I'd ask to sit with sales, customer success, and maybe someone from finance to map the funnel from first touch through renewal. I'd want to know how you define a good customer, what it costs to win them, and where we lose them. Then I'd come back to you with a simple sketch of the money flows and ask what I got wrong."

He raised an eyebrow. "Why?"

"Because I don't want to be the marketer who speaks only in impressions and followers," Anthony said. "I want to sit in this room and talk about lifetime value and payback as if it's my native language. I don't know it yet—but I know how to learn it."

The finance director jotted a note. "All right," he said. "Next question. Tell me about a time you had no idea what you were doing at work and what you did about it."

Anthony laughed. "Only one time?"

He told him about his first internship, when he was handed a marketing automation platform he'd never seen. He could have pretended to know it. Instead, he blocked out an hour every morning for two weeks, watched tutorials, joined a user group, and DM'd people on LinkedIn who listed the tool in their profiles.

"I kept a 'dumb questions' notebook," he said. "When I hit a wall, I'd take that list to a more senior teammate. It was my way of saying, 'I did my homework—now can you fill in the gaps?' "

The finance director leaned back.

"So you're comfortable not knowing," he said.

"I'm not comfortable," Anthony replied. "But I'm willing to sit with that discomfort as long as I'm moving forward."

He smiled for the first time.

"Last thing," he said. "Most recent thing you learned that had nothing to do with marketing."

"Basic SQL," he said. "I wanted to stop waiting in line for reports. I'm terrible at it right now, but I can pull my own simple data instead of bothering the analyst every time."

The finance director closed his notebook.

"Thank you, Anthony. That's all I need."

Walking out, he replayed the conversation. He hadn't dazzled anyone with financial jargon. He'd admitted his gaps out loud to the person who controlled the budget.

On the subway home, the mental fences rose again:

- *You should've known the revenue model.*
- *You're not analytical enough.*
- *Real marketers have this figured out already.*

Then he heard another voice, quieter but steadier:

- *You told the truth.*
- *You showed how you learn.*
- *You asked to be judged on your trajectory, not just your transcript.*

A week later, the email arrived.

The subject line read, "Offer: Marketing Intern."

The body was short.

"We're still not sure you're 'work-ready' in the traditional sense, but your curiosity and learning plan convinced us you will be. If you're willing to treat this summer as an intense learning sprint, we're willing to invest in you."

Anthony didn't have all the skills yet.

He had something more powerful: a thirst to learn, and leaders willing to pour into it.

Learning Agility: The Advantage Employers Notice

Anthony is fictional, but the situation isn't.

Throughout the interviews for this book, senior leaders, marketers, and hiring managers kept returning to the same point: they would rather hire someone eager to learn than someone who acts as if they already know everything.

In human resources language, that quality is called learning agility. It matters because employers are not only hiring for what you can do on day one. They are also judging how quickly you can grow as skills change. Harvard Business Review highlighted Gartner research showing that only 29 percent of hiring managers said their last hire arrived highly prepared for the current role, let alone how the role would evolve (Harvard Business Review, 2021).

Advice From Leaders Who Hire Marketers

Debbie Gainsford, an Australian marketing consultant who built her career without a formal degree, told me, "Some people think you need that degree to get started, but for me, finding people who believed in me and having leaders who supported my growth on the job has been so important." What helped her early on, she explained, wasn't textbook knowledge but her approach to problems: "My mindset and my way of thinking mattered more than knowing every framework."

Gainsford's big break came at Getty Images. "I joined them the day they went 100 percent digital, and they had only 200 images on the website," she said. "Getty needed someone who could learn quickly during a moment of reinvention, and I thrive in environments where ambiguity and disruption are present."

What made her stand out wasn't perfection; it was her willingness to stretch. "I'm an introvert at heart, and I had to learn to step outside my comfort zone."

Staci Lynn, a chief operating officer at a healthcare company, said, "I started as a receptionist. One thing I always did in my career was learn everything I could about whatever I was working on. Part of that was getting exposure to people and raising my hand to say, 'Hey, I'd like to learn more about this.' It was a way to help lighten someone else's load and to build my skill set so I could be more valuable to an organization in the future. You have to do some of the hard work and the grind to learn and grow . . . it makes you a better team member for the organization."

Josh King, a former naval officer, said his passion for learning began during his time in the U.S. Navy. "I started raising my hand and volunteering for everything, and I quickly mastered them. I studied every night. I understood how important it was for me to learn how the whole ship operated, and that it would make me a better officer."

That hunger for knowledge arose from adversity. King was training to be a Navy pilot when inner ear problems derailed his flight career. After the attacks of September 11, 2001, he was reassigned to an aircraft carrier. "I was miserable," he recalled. "I went from flying at hundreds of knots per hour to just twenty-five miles an hour." Instead of coasting, King doubled down. "I volunteered for the hardest jobs on the ship that nobody else wanted, and I mastered them in a short period of time."

The result? Pacific Fleet Ship Handler of the Year. "I succeeded, not because I'm any smarter than the guy who went to Harvard or MIT, because I'm not, but because I knew how serious it would be for me to understand the entire workings of the ship."

Now, as vice president of strategic initiatives for a medical equipment manufacturer, King believes that same orientation separates those who advance from those who plateau. "Nobody expects you to have answers. What would delight them is well-thought-out questions."

What Hiring Data Reveals About Entry-Level Marketers

The market expects you to learn quickly after school—and to enjoy the process. The problem? Most education systems are not designed to develop learning agility.

Content analyses of marketing job ads show employers prize motivation, adaptability, and willingness to learn alongside technical tools—with 75% of entry-level listings now requiring analytical skills (McArthur et al., 2017; Schlee & Karns, 2017).

Yet a stubborn gap persists: surveys of employers and recent graduates find that new hires struggle with ambiguity, avoid open-ended problems, and prefer step-by-step instructions (Hickman & Stoica, 2023; Mercado & Mercado, 2025).

We see this tension playing out in hiring data. Marketing roles are shifting toward growth, product, and performance specialties—where 68% of marketers say landing a job feels harder than five years ago (Karlovitch, 2024; Taligence, 2025).

The market is splitting into a K-shape: senior and specialized roles grew 17.6% year-over-year, while entry-level openings declined 4.5% (Taligence, 2025). The ladder isn't broken—but the bottom rungs are crowded, and the gaps between them are widening.

What's driving the squeeze? Partly AI. Three in four marketers say they need to master specialized niche skills to stay relevant as automation reshapes the field (Karlovitch, 2024). The tools keep changing. The expectations keep rising. Standing still means falling behind.

When entry-level doors narrow, the people who keep moving are those who

- Notice where demand is growing
- Teach themselves new skills quickly
- Show employers they can figure things out

That's what this "T" in T-GROWTH is about. The thirst to learn is not a trivial trait.

It's a survival skill, a strategic advantage, and the foundation for every other letter in this framework. Without it, grit hardens into stubbornness, tech fluency devolves into tool chasing, and wisdom never has a chance to take shape.

Using Design Thinking to Build Business Acumen

Thirst to learn is essential—but learning *what*? Anthony's moment with the finance leader reveals a critical gap many early-career marketers face: understanding the "why" behind their work. Technical skills get you in the door; business acumen earns you a seat at the table.

Fortunately, there's a proven framework for cultivating this curiosity—one that transforms vague questions into structured inquiry.

Design Thinking for Building Business Acumen

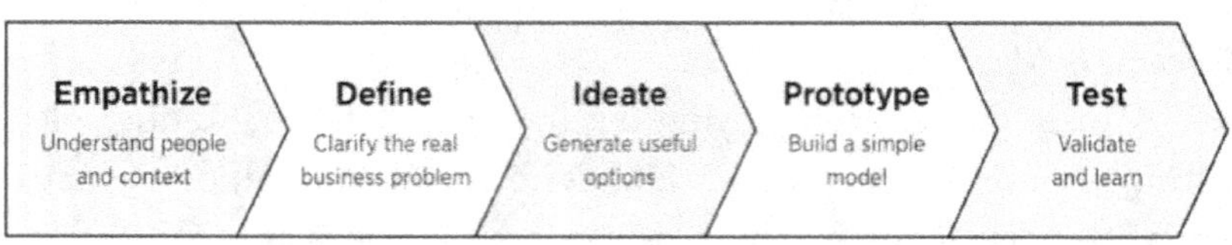

Figure 1 Connecting Marketing Work to Business Outcomes

What is Design Thinking?

Design thinking originated from Stanford's d.school (Hasso Plattner Institute of Design), led by David Kelley and colleagues in the early 2000s. Initially created to solve complex product design problems, the approach—empathize, define, ideate, prototype, and test—has become vital for solving business issues across various fields. Companies like IDEO, Intuit, and IBM have embraced design thinking to drive innovation and focus on the customer throughout their organizations.

Empathize: Interview Your Internal Customers. Before your next interview or Monday morning meeting, conduct empathy interviews with colleagues in finance, sales, and operations. Ask open-ended questions: "Walk me through how a customer becomes profitable for us," or "What keeps you up at night about our revenue model?" You're expanding your understanding of the business from multiple perspectives, just as you would research customer personas.

Define: Reframe the Problem Statement. Anthony knew the brand story but overlooked the business story. Instead of asking, "What are our marketing tactics?" ask "What business problem does this campaign solve?" Write problem statements that connect marketing efforts to revenue, retention, or margin growth.

Ideate: Generate Business-Relevant Options. Once you understand the people involved and have reframed the business problem, start generating possible solutions. Don't stop at the first campaign idea or channel tactic. Ask, "What are three different ways marketing could help solve this problem?" Maybe the answer is better messaging, a sales enablement tool, a customer education sequence, or a retention play. Ideation helps you move from "I have an assignment" to "I can create options." That's where business acumen starts to show up—when you can connect creativity to trade-offs, resources, and outcomes.

Prototype: Model Your Business Hypotheses. Create simple one-page business models for campaigns before launch. Map the customer journey to revenue touchpoints. Show how awareness translates into consideration, conversion, and lifetime value. Share these with cross-functional peers for feedback before committing resources.

Test: Reverse Engineer Results. Take your company's annual report or investor deck. Reverse engineer it:

- How does each revenue line connect to marketing activities?
- Which customer segments drive profitability?
- Where do margins compress?

When you demonstrate curiosity about the business model, take initiative to understand the financial mechanics, and show an affinity for solving profit problems—not just marketing problems—you become indispensable.

The next time someone asks, "How does this company make money?" you'll have an answer.

Making Moves as Mini T-Shaped Building Experiments

In street slang, "making moves" means taking action to improve your circumstances—hustling with purpose. That's exactly what this section covers.

Design thinking gives you frameworks for big problems, but real growth happens in the small experiments you run every day. The Moves that follow work like mini design sprints—quick actions you can test, adapt, and apply to your own situation.

Each Move is a chance to practice curiosity, build skills, and learn your way forward. You'll find a Moves section at the end of every chapter in this book, offering practical ways to put each concept into action right away. Don't just read about learning agility—make moves.

Move 1: Improve Your Listening Skills

"Active listening is more than waiting for your turn to speak. It's the core skill that separates forgettable marketers from trusted partners," said Jillian Vorce, Founder of The Jillian Group, which comprises a portfolio of ventures and strategic services.

Vorce explained that real opportunities come from taking the time to *truly listen to other*s. "Active listening once landed me on a TEDx stage, not because I was the loudest voice, but because I created space for others. So many opportunities come from active listening," Vorce explained.

In her speech, Vorce illustrates what active listening looks like. "After sharing something vulnerable with a new acquaintance, I faced a long, uncomfortable silence. Rather than rushing to fill it, I sat with it, keeping the space open and waiting for my friend to rejoin the conversation." That's active listening. Resisting the urge to jump in, staying present with discomfort, and allowing the other person to process.

Early-career marketers often rush to offer solutions, especially when trying to prove themselves. However, prescribing too quickly can make you lose sight of the real problem, the actual person, and the genuine opportunity. "Listening before you prescribe means noticing what someone *isn't* saying and asking a follow-up question that shows you care about their world, not just your task list. When you listen this way, people *tell* you everything you need to know," said Vorce.

> **Ask AI for Help:** Prompt AI to think as an executive coach helping an early-career marketer improve active listening. I recently had a conversation with [person/role] about [topic]. My goal in the conversation was [goal]. I felt the urge to jump in when [describe moment]. Here is what I remember saying: [brief summary]. Here is what the other person said or seemed to signal: [brief summary].
>
> Please help me review the conversation. Create a simple table with four columns:
>
> - A moment where I may have spoken too soon
> - What the other person may have been signaling
> - What I could have listened for
> - A better follow-up question I could ask next time
>
> Do not assume you know what the other person meant. Focus on possibilities and better questions. Then give me three follow-up questions I can practice using in my next conversation.

Move 2: Learn How Money Moves in Your Company

If you want to sharpen your T-shaped skills, you must understand a key truth that James Furbush emphasized: "Business runs on money, and marketers who understand how it flows instantly gain credibility." Furbush has spent over a decade in healthcare marketing, moving from content roles to VP of marketing at multiple healthcare SaaS companies. That journey taught him something essential: "You can't walk into a room with a CFO or someone in finance and not understand a P&L or how budgets are made. When you ask for a budget, finance wants to know: What is the return on that investment?"

Furbush emphasized that understanding money isn't just about marketing; it's about knowing who truly controls the purse strings. If you're backed by venture capital or private equity, "It's not just the board you need to understand. You also need to understand who controls the purse strings behind the board and what they want to see." This level of business insight is crucial: "Because at the end of the day, companies spend money and make money, and you have to understand how all those levers are measured."

When you learn to speak finance, you stop sounding like "just marketing" and start sounding like a business partner.

> **Ask AI for Help:** Prompt AI to act as a CFO coaching an early-career marketer. Tell it about your company, role, target customers, and your best guess for how the company makes money. Ask it to map how money likely moves through the business: revenue sources, major costs, margin drivers, how marketing spend may be judged, and what finance may need before approving the budget. Tell AI not to invent company-specific financial data. Then ask for three common marketer misunderstandings and five smart questions to bring to finance, sales, or product.

Move 3: Study Job Posts Like a Researcher

Here's a practice I use and recommend: Treat job postings as data. When you analyze job postings systematically, you start to see what the market truly values, not just what people *say* they value. Insights from recruiting firms and other analysts show a rise in hybrid roles that combine growth, product, analytics, and customer understanding.

Once a month, I review about 20 job listings from different companies and note the skills, tools, and responsibilities that recur. This simple habit gives me a real-time view of emerging expectations. Then I turn those insights into small learning sprints—micro-projects that allow me to focus on practicing one skill at a time. Over time, this process helps me develop a sharper, more adaptable T-shape. I'm not guessing what matters; I'm learning directly from the market.

> **Ask AI for Help:** Prompt AI to assume the role of a labor market analyst. Request that AI evaluate several job descriptions for common skills, tools, and responsibilities. Explain what these patterns reveal about what employers truly value. Paste multiple job descriptions for roles you're interested in, even if they seem repetitive. Use the insights to select one skill to focus on next, then design and complete a small micro-project that allows you to learn directly from the market.

Move 4: Become the Most Prepared Person in the Room

"I came in on my first day, thinking that I was, you know, inexperienced and didn't know much. But I knew more about product management than the people working there." Chris Walker describes what happened when he prepared relentlessly before starting a role he'd never done before.

Walker is an engineer who transitioned into marketing and eventually became a three-time founder, building Refine Labs, Passetto, and earlier ventures that shaped his approach to learning and performance. Early in your career, effort matters more than experience.

Before his first product management role, Walker read books, took courses, and learned from experts. He took on roles he wasn't "qualified" for and outperformed others with years of experience by preparing more thoroughly. "It requires substantial effort from the most prepared person in the room, and most people aren't willing to do that. If you are, it gives you a huge advantage."

When you read, listen, study, and practice on your own time, you close the experience gap faster than any employer can train you. Preparation is the great equalizer.

> **Ask AI for Help:** Prompt AI to assume the role of a professional coach to help you identify what a strong performer in the role you seek already understands, then build a short, focused preparation plan around those gaps. Provide context about the role, project, or situation you're stepping into and where you feel least prepared.

Move 5: Immerse Yourself in a Topic

"You need to understand human behavior. If you grasp the decision-making shortcuts people rely on, you'll be able to craft marketing messages that are more likely to be noticed, understood, acted upon, and remembered," said Nancy Harhut, co-founder and chief creative officer at HBT Marketing and the author of the award-winning *book Using Behavioral Science in Marketing.* Named one of the "10 Most Fascinating People in B2B Marketing," she has built her career by blending behavioral science with marketing strategy.

Harhut's journey began when a mentor recommended Robert Cialdini's Influence. "I became a convert. I started making margin notes and underlining passages," thinking about how the principles could solve her clients' challenges. She tested ideas, observed results, and gained confidence with each experiment.

That approach paid off greatly when she applied a behavioral principle called the "pull of the magnetic middle" to a struggling client campaign—resulting in a 459% increase over the control group. "It made me feel that I was right to follow my passion," she reflected, "that I was right to stand up and have the courage of my convictions."

Ask AI for Help: Prompt AI to assume the role of a professional coach, naming the topic you want to investigate in depth and why it matters to your work right now. Ask AI to help you identify the core ideas to focus on first and to design a simple plan that mixes reading with real-world testing. Use one experiment to apply what you're learning, then reflect on what changed in your thinking or results.

Move 6: Stay Curious About What's Next

"AI forces us to become more strategic and more authentically human," remarked Liza Adams, an AI advisor, fractional CMO, and one of Pavilion's Go-to-Market community's 50 CMOs to Watch in 2024. Her journey demonstrates that technology rewards those who stay curious, not those who wait for perfect certainty.

Adams didn't immediately drive her team toward mastery. Instead, she encouraged small experiments, learning through action, and sharing insights. "Think big. Start small. Move fast," she emphasized. "Don't let perfect be the enemy of the good. No one knows what 'perfect' looks like anyway. But as we move forward, we learn from the market. We iterate and keep improving."

Her warning is equally clear: "If we don't take control of this narrative, someone else will create one for us." When others view marketers as tacticians, they question whether we belong at the decision-making table or if we are needed at all.

For early-career marketers, curiosity is your advantage. Explore what's emerging, stay adaptable, and prove your strategic value before someone else defines your role.

Ask AI for Help: Prompt AI to gather a virtual panel of advisors with diverse viewpoints, including strategy, finance, customer, creativity, technology, leadership, and one wildcard. I want the panel to assist you in thinking through a decision-making process, asking a few clarifying questions before they give their input. Use their insights to identify where perspectives align, where tradeoffs are present, and choose one next step to test instead of waiting for certainty.

Move 7: Turn Your School Projects Into Proof of Talent

"I was thinking, *what can I do right now to stand out from the 200 other people I'll be competing against?*" said Alexandra Lazarenko, a licensed financial services professional at Charles Schwab and, on LinkedIn, the self-named "Poll Lady."

As a student, Lazarenko decided that every paper and side project could serve as evidence of her thinking. During school breaks, she wrote detailed reports—similar to day-trading analyses based on interviews with professional traders—and posted them on LinkedIn as projects. "These projects helped me bridge the gap from college to the corporate world," she said. "I wanted recruiters to see that I'm willing to learn and go above and beyond, even if I don't yet know every detail of the role."

She combined those projects with daily LinkedIn polls on trends and consumer behavior. Her goal: 1,000 polls in a row. "It's a labor of love, but there have been real-world impacts," she explained. Colleagues now see her as the person who shows up, asks smart questions, and turns curiosity into visible work. That's what your projects can be too—not homework, but proof.

Ask AI for Help: Prompt AI to think like a recruiter and career coach. Have AI help review one or more of your school projects and translate that work into evidence of real-world skills by highlighting the decisions you made, the abilities you demonstrated, and where you went beyond the assignment. For context, explain your school project, assignment, or side project. Use this output to craft a concise, LinkedIn-ready project description that demonstrates your readiness for professional responsibility—and consider one way to extend the project to make it even stronger proof. For additional perspective, ask the recruiter to critically review your LinkedIn post to ensure it aligns with their client's needs.

Epilogue: Anthony Starts Asking Better Questions

By the end of his internship, Anthony's title hadn't changed, but his understanding had.

He could now easily sketch the company's revenue model on a whiteboard without needing notes. He understood which segments were the most profitable, which channels generated the highest lifetime value, and where customers typically dropped out of the process.

He still wasn't the loudest voice in the meetings.

But when the CFO asked, "If we cut this campaign, what happens to margin next quarter?" he no longer panicked. He pulled up a simple chart linking past investments to retention, explained the assumptions, and suggested a small test instead of a full cut.

His slides weren't the prettiest in the room. They were the ones people kept.

When a friend from school called to complain that their first job was "beneath them," Anthony thought of all the professionals in this chapter.

He realized something. The real gap wasn't between school and work. It was between expecting to be taught and choosing to learn. That choice had already begun to change his career. It can change yours, too.

Works Cited

Harvard Business Review. (2021, March-April). Reengineering the recruitment process. Harvard Business Review.

Hickman, T., & Stoica, M. (2023). Employer's perception of new hires: What determines their overall satisfaction with recent graduates? The Journal of Research in Business Education, 63(1), 6-23.

Interaction Design Foundation. (2025). What is design thinking? Interaction Design Foundation.

Karlovitch, S. (2024, October 25). The marketing job market: Here's what the numbers say. Marketing Dive.

McArthur, E., Kubacki, K., Pang, B., & Alcaraz, C. (2017). The employers' view of "work-ready" graduates: A study of advertisements for marketing jobs in Australia. Journal of Marketing Education, 39(2), 82-93.

Mercado, J. O., & Mercado, R. E. (2025). Gap analysis of unemployed business graduates' employability skills and industry preferences. Scientific International (Lahore), 37(2), 95-102.

Schlee, R. P., & Karns, G. L. (2017). Job requirements for marketing graduates: Are there differences in the knowledge, skills, and personal attributes needed for different salary levels?

Journal of Marketing Education, 39(2), 69-81.

Taligence & Aspen Technology Labs. (2025). U.S. marketing jobs report: Q1 2025. Taligence.

CHAPTER 3: GRIT & INTEGRITY

"Do not get lost in a sea of despair. Be hopeful, be optimistic. Our struggle is not the struggle of a day, a week, a month, or a year—it is the struggle of a lifetime."
—John Lewis

Field Story: The Green Arrows

Nala thought the day was over.

She had survived the launch meeting, negotiated last-minute copy adjustments, and finally delivered a clean dashboard from the analytics tool. Her first major campaign as an associate brand manager wasn't a disaster, but it wasn't a victory either.

Runners loved the new sports drink. Casual gym-goers hardly noticed it. Students complained about the price.

She reviewed the performance report again. Same story. A few strong segments, a few weaker ones. Tests were still ongoing.

At 7:41 p.m., an email appeared: *"Need your slides tonight for the board pre-read. Keep it simple—green arrows up to keep everyone aligned. —Matt, VP of Sales."*

Green arrows.

Nala examined the charts with flat regions and noisy data. By applying the right filters, she could make the story clear and impressive. Highlight the top segments. Remove the weaker ones. Smooth out the dip in week three.

No one was pressuring her to lie. They just weren't asking for the full truth either.

The office around her had become quiet. A cleaning cart rattled past her desk. Her friends were already texting about dinner plans.

You're overthinking this, she told herself. Everybody polishes the story. Isn't that how the game was played?

She inserted the "Top Markets" chart into a slide. It looked good. Engagement increased. Conversions increased. A clear upward trend. If she only sent this, the board would see what they wanted: progress and potential.

Her cursor hovered over the export button.

A different thought interrupted, quieter but more piercing. If the board acted on this, would she trust herself later?

Nala closed the slide and opened a blank email instead.

Hi Matt, I'm gathering our top results, but there are early warning signs we should address as well: student pushback on pricing, a few underperforming regions, and tests that still need more time. Could we connect for ten minutes before I finalize everything? I want tomorrow's discussion to be accurate and productive.

She read the message twice. Sending it indicated she was asking a VP to slow down. It suggested she might be labeled as difficult or overly cautious. It showed she prioritized accuracy over praise.

Her heart thumped. She hit *Send.*

Stepping into the cold night air, she had no idea whether tomorrow would reveal she had made a brave choice or a foolish one.

On the train home, the mental fences showed up right on time:

- *You should have kept it simple.*
- *You're too new to push back.*
- *Real leaders know how to play the game.*

Then another inside voice answered back, quieter but steadier:

- *You told the truth.*
- *You showed how you think.*

- *You asked to be judged on your integrity, not just your slides.*

She did not know it yet, but that small email was the beginning of a reputation.

Build Credibility Through Grit and Integrity

If you've ever examined a report that told two different stories depending on the filters you used—and felt drawn toward the version that made your work look better—you already know the choice this chapter discusses.

What Nala experienced in that quiet office is the same crossroads leaders repeatedly described to me during interviews: the point when comfort and credibility pull in opposite directions.

This chapter examines the two traits leaders trust most: grit and integrity. Every story, study, and move in these pages ties back to the moments when they matter most.

Grit is the dedication to keep going when work is tough, confusing, or slow. Integrity is the self-control to tell the truth and do what's right, especially when there's pressure to do otherwise. Together, they send a clear message: *You can rely on me to act responsibly.*

The uncomfortable truth is that telling the truth can cost you in the short run. The even tougher truth is that not telling it costs you more over time.

Advice From Leaders Who Hire and Promote Marketers

They came from different industries, different backgrounds, and different points in their careers. But when I asked what actually earns the trust required for larger opportunities, they kept arriving at the same place.

Josh King, a former naval officer and VP of marketing, starts every failure the same way: "If something goes wrong, my first question is always: What could I have done differently?" Not blame. Ownership. Over time, that habit makes teams less defensive, more honest, and more willing to learn.

Debbie Gainsford built a global marketing career without a formal degree. For her, grit isn't about working until you collapse. "It's okay to switch off — we're in marketing, not saving lives." Steady, sustainable effort beats heroic burnout every time.

Aaron Hassen, co-founder of Aaron Hassen Marketing, measures every decision against one question: "If this were my money, would I still make this choice?" His advice to early-career marketers is equally direct: "Think like an owner."

Bob Moesta, co-creator of the Jobs-to-Be-Done framework, calculated how many times he'd likely see his adult children before he died. The number was twenty-eight. Not years — visits. He immediately fired the clients who wasted his time and started protecting what remained. You may feel like time is the one thing you have plenty of right now. But the habit Bob describes — deciding in advance what your time is *for* — is something you can build now, long before the arithmetic gets urgent.

Staci Lynn, a COO in senior care, defines both grit and integrity in the same breath. When hurricanes hit, she flies down and sleeps on the floor alongside her team. That's grit — not the kind you put on a résumé, but the kind that shows up at 2 a.m. because the work demands it. On integrity, she doesn't hedge: "The quickest way to get terminated is to lack integrity and lie about what you're doing all day long." Her guiding principle is simple: "Do the right thing, and the bottom line will take care of itself."

Face what is real. Stay in the fight. Protect trust. These aren't soft ideas; they are supported by data too.

What the Data Reveals About Work Readiness

Here's what nobody in a job interview will tell you: the leaders you've just heard from aren't describing a high bar. They're describing the baseline. And the data shows most people entering the profession aren't meeting it.

A 2025 national survey of employers found that for competencies like professionalism and leadership, the gap between what employers expect and what they see in recent graduates exceeds 30 percentage points (National Association of Colleges and Employers, 2025).

Meanwhile, surveys of recent graduates show rising anxiety about whether their degree prepared them for meaningful work at all (Cengage Group, 2023; ZipRecruiter, 2023). Low employer confidence. High self-doubt. That combination doesn't just feel bad — it creates a fragile starting point when real pressure arrives.

Studies of marketing job postings reveal that employers often look for qualities like work ethic, time management, reliability, and accountability.

These are simple words, but they imply something deeper. Employers want to know: Will you show up, follow through, and be honest when work gets challenging?

Job market reports reveal another layer. Senior marketing roles—such as director, vice president, and C-level positions—have grown more quickly than many entry-level roles. Organizations are investing in individuals who can handle ambiguity, lead teams, and make principled decisions about data, AI, and customer impact. Meanwhile, some employers openly admit they are hesitant to hire recent graduates because they worry about professionalism and resilience.

The pattern is clear. The market doubts graduates' readiness but still seeks leaders who demonstrate resilience, accountability, and honest judgment. Translation: The person interviewing you probably already questions whether you can handle tough feedback, stay calm under pressure, or admit when something isn't working. That is the gap this chapter aims to help you close. These employer expectations closely align with what psychologists have discovered about who succeeds in demanding environments.

Talent Got You Here. It Won't Keep You Here.

Here's an interesting fact about marketing careers: Talent alone doesn't determine who lasts.

Psychologist Angela Duckworth studied individuals who complete challenging tasks: West Point cadets, spelling bee winners, first-year teachers in tough schools, and salespeople hitting quotas. Her discovery is now widely known: the best predictor isn't IQ, social intelligence, or physical strength. It is grit, which she describes as passion and perseverance toward long-term goals (Duckworth, 2016).

But "long-term" carries the main meaning in that sentence. Duckworth isn't referring to completing a campaign or getting through a tough quarter. She's talking about people who stay on a path for years, pushing through times when work feels dull, progress seems invisible, and quitting seems sensible. Grit explains why some marketers develop real expertise over a decade, while others, equally talented, drift from one eighteen-month stint to another.

What makes someone gritty? Duckworth highlights four psychological qualities that develop over time. **Interest** keeps you engaged long enough to improve — you care about the work itself, not just the results. **Deliberate practice** involves working on the difficult parts, not just repeating what's easy. **Purpose** connects your daily tasks to something bigger than just your own progress. **Hope** isn't wishful thinking; it's the belief that your effort can change your situation, especially when results haven't appeared yet.

The good news: Grit isn't something you're born with. You develop it by nurturing your curiosity in your field, setting aside regular practice time each week, linking your work to something bigger than yourself, and training yourself to ask "What can I learn?" when facing failure instead of "What's wrong with me?"

But perseverance alone doesn't explain how people stay honest with themselves when reality becomes uncomfortable, and that's where grit becomes more complex and fascinating. Admiral James Stockdale spent over seven years as a prisoner of war in Vietnam. He was tortured, isolated, and kept without any set release date. Years later, author Jim Collins interviewed Stockdale for his influential study on why some companies succeed and others excel (Collins, 2001). Collins wasn't looking for military heroes — he was seeking a framework to explain why some organizations thrive through adversity while others fall apart.

Stockdale's answer became one of the most lasting ideas in Collins's work, a concept he called "The Stockdale Paradox": "You must never confuse faith that you will prevail in the end with the discipline to confront the most brutal facts of your current reality." What struck Collins most was Stockdale's observation about who didn't survive the camps. It wasn't the pessimists — it was the optimists, the ones who kept saying, "We'll be out by Christmas." Christmas would pass. "By Easter." Easter would pass. Each broken expectation wore them down. They weren't lacking hope — they were lacking the habit of facing reality. Their optimism became a way to avoid the truth, and when the truth finally caught up, they had nothing left.

The Stockdale Paradox adds a crucial element to Duckworth's framework. Grit isn't just perseverance driven by optimism. It's the ability to hold two seemingly opposing ideas simultaneously: unwavering confidence that you will figure this out over time, and brutal honesty about what isn't working right now.

For early-career marketers, the message is clear: Toxic positivity can harm you. The campaigns that didn't meet expectations, the metrics that aren't progressing, the feedback that stings — these aren't hurdles to your growth. They are the foundational elements. The discipline to face them honestly, without spin or self-protection, distinguishes those who improve from those who merely survive.

Collins extended this individual principle to the organizational level. In companies that transitioned from good to great and maintained that performance for fifteen years or more, leaders created cultures where employees could report bad news — such as failing products, weak results, or internal issues — without fear. They didn't punish the messengers. At the same time, they trusted that the organization would eventually succeed amid tough markets and necessary pivots. The research showed this wasn't just a personality trait of individual leaders — it was a practice embedded in how the organization operates.

Together, these three perspectives of Duckworth, Stockdale, and Collins form a continuum. Duckworth shows how individuals persist through the long process of developing skills. Stockdale illustrates how leaders endure extreme uncertainty without losing their grip on reality. Collins explains how organizations that face honest confrontation outperform others over decades.

The core message for you: Grit isn't an innate trait you either possess or lack. It's a collection of learnable habits. Cultivate a sincere interest in your craft. Incorporate deliberate practice into your daily routine. Connect your work to a purpose beyond just promotion. Train yourself to respond to setbacks with curiosity instead of self-criticism. Most importantly, develop the discipline to face what's really true about your situation—the weaknesses, the gaps, the uncomfortable feedback—while holding onto the belief that you will figure this out if you keep pushing forward.

Frameworks are helpful, but they become truly effective only when turned into small, repeatable habits—exactly what the Moves in this chapter aim to help you build.

Using the Grit Continuum to Guide Your Career

Nala's moment with the "green arrows" email demonstrates all three levels. At the individual level, she needs resilience: the willingness to stay in discomfort, risk appearing less polished, and keep learning from imperfect results.

At the individual leadership level, she applies the Stockdale Paradox. She refuses to ignore harsh realities while staying hopeful about a way forward. At the organizational level, she communicates a clear message. She acts like someone who helps companies move from wishful thinking to honest execution.

You will encounter your own version of this scene. A client might ask you to smooth over a weak test result. A manager could push vanity metrics over meaningful ones. A job search might last longer than you expected. A project you championed could stumble in public.

In those moments, grit and integrity aren't shown through grand speeches. They are shown in small actions:

- You tell the truth about the numbers
- You own your part in what happened
- You protect your energy instead of burning out
- You ask the hard question no one else wants to ask
- You keep showing up when no one is applauding

The Moves that follow are designed to help you practice those habits in small, repeatable ways.

Moves: Practice Grit and Integrity at Work

In the previous chapter, design thinking offered a framework for understanding business problems. Here, the Grit Continuum provides a framework for how you show up as those challenges arise.

Think of each move as a small experiment. None of them need permission or a special job title. They are simple actions you can practice during school projects, internships, first jobs, and side hustles. Over time, these actions help build your personal brand: someone who faces reality, stays committed, and can be trusted with greater responsibilities.

Move 8: Show Ownership Before You're Given Authority

"I started with nothing on my résumé that would get me hired, so ownership was all I had," said Aaron Hassen, founder of AH Marketing and a long-time adviser to early-career marketers. His path didn't begin with degrees or internships—it started with necessity. "When you don't have the credentials, networking and performance become your only leverage," he explained.

Hassen shares a truth many miss: Grit often starts as survival. "My resume alone wasn't going to get me the job, but someone's trust in me could." So he did what few new marketers are willing to do—he asked founders for a chance to help, promised to think like an owner, and delivered results. That dedication doubled revenue at his first startup within a year.

Hassen's Think Like an Owner perspective continues to influence how he evaluates talent. "I don't need you to have every skill on day one. What I want to see is passion, attitude, willingness to learn, and the ability to take initiative," he said. Degrees matter much less than demonstrating you can reduce a hiring manager's risk. That's why he advises early-career marketers to take on small projects—even unpaid ones—to prove themselves. "Stepping through the door for free doesn't mean you're free forever. It means you're willing to do the work before you're given the title."

Early-career marketers often wait for permission—permission to start, contribute, and lead. However, waiting rarely builds trust. "You can't come to the table with answers before you understand the business," Hassen said. "Ask questions that reveal your intentions. Show humility. Think like an owner from day one." That's grit in action: doing the unglamorous work that proves your value long before anyone officially recognizes it.

> **Ask AI for Help:** Prompt AI to think like a business executive who teaches the mindset of ownership of outcomes to business students. Ask AI to teach you how you would think about your project. For context, I am currently working on (describe your project). Use AI to identify potential risks you can reduce and to design a short, 7-day sprint that demonstrates initiative before you're asked. Take one action from that sprint and make it visible.

Move 9: Reframe Problems to Unlock Step-Change Results

Ownership is one form of grit, but another emerges when you are willing to think beyond the constraints in front of you.

Angela Paules, a marketing leader known for creating exceptional consumer campaigns, shares a story about a junior marketer on her team who showed real grit. The team was working on a swim-safety campaign for children, but something wasn't clicking. Kids weren't paying attention. Instead of accepting the limitations of a small brand, this junior marketer asked a much bigger question. Angela recalled, "She saw something missing and had the courage to ask: What if we partnered with Hasbro?"

For those unfamiliar, Hasbro is a global entertainment giant responsible for some of the most recognizable brands in toys, games, and children's media—such as Monopoly, Transformers, and popular animated characters like Peppa Pig. Partnering with a company of that size would be a long shot for any small brand.

The junior marketer had a clear vision: licensing Peppa Pig, the cheerful cartoon character loved by preschoolers around the world, to make swim safety feel fun and familiar instead of like a lecture. She didn't wait for permission. She researched alignment, drafted a pitch, and sent it cold. According to Paules, "The marketer did that fearlessly, and her approach wasn't reckless. It was intentional. She was thoughtful. She listened carefully. She respected every part of the process."

When Hasbro responded, the real test started. Licensing requirements. Creative standards. Tight deadlines. Multiple review rounds. But she stayed steady. Angela said, "She really shot for the stars. She wasn't afraid to make it happen."

What stood out wasn't the idea; it was how she carried it out. "She earned their trust one detail at a time," Angela said. That's early-career grit: one bold step, supported by consistent, professional follow-through.

> **Ask AI for Help:** Prompt AI to act as a strategic coach who assists early-career marketers in thinking beyond constraints without overstepping authority. Have it reframe your current project by analyzing the target audience, identifying the gap, and recognizing the resources you truly control. Use this output to turn one bold idea into a small, low-risk experiment you can propose and carry out, then focus on disciplined execution to build trust.

Move 10: Stay Solid When Things Get Chaotic

Big ideas matter, but grit also appears in the everyday chaos—when the work feels messy, reactive, or overwhelming.

"Remain positive on purpose" is the mantra Robin Bowling, a healthcare technology CMO, repeats to herself and her team. When she joined her current company, the marketing group was broken. "People were crying in meetings," she recalled. "They felt they had no ability to say no."

Robin didn't jump in with a big plan. She began with an honest chat. Using a simple stop–start–continue exercise, she asked, "What's working? What would you change? What do we need to stop doing?" When the team admitted they were overwhelmed with reactive requests, she took action.

Robin met with every C-suite leader and introduced a new way of working: a shared request system, an agile backlog, and a clear, service-level agreement. "I told my team, 'You can push back. If there's a problem, you come to me.'" Over time, that once-defeated group became the company's highest-performing team.

Her idea of grit isn't loud hustle. It's calm, steady leadership, listening intently, setting boundaries, and deliberately choosing positivity, especially when a team is nearly ready to give up.

> **Ask AI for Help:** Prompt AI to think like an experienced leadership coach. Describe a real project or team dynamic where you feel overwhelmed or reactive. Ask AI to clarify your intention, identify two or three consistent behaviors that reflect your values, and design a simple system to reset expectations and set professional boundaries. Use the output to practice one script for saying no or redirecting requests, then track your consistency for two weeks to see whether you're showing up with calm, disciplined grit.

Move 11: Grow Your Capacity Through Chosen Discomfort

Staying steady is one kind of strength, but another comes from deliberately choosing discomfort and allowing it to grow your abilities.

Angela Carrasco didn't aim to develop grit. She aimed to be honest. "I was highlighting a book I was reading and adding all my little sticky notes, but I had to ask myself—what are you doing with this information? It's beautiful in your sticky notes, but where's the action?"

Two weeks later, Angela was unexpectedly laid off. The shock made her face how much she'd been living in comfort—steady job, stable routine, predictable days. "I thought, okay, enough procrastinating. What is the most uncomfortable thing you can think of doing today?"

That question inspired her 100-day Discomfort Project: a pledge to do one thing each day that challenged her emotionally, socially, or professionally. Some days involved reaching out to someone she admired. On other days, she had to say yes to something she normally avoided or she tried something she wasn't good at. "It was very inquisitive," Angela said. "Where is this going to take me? What things am I going to find out about myself that I wouldn't if I went the expected route?"

Instead of letting fear shrink her world, she used discomfort to expand it, one small, chosen challenge at a time.

> **Ask AI for Help:** Prompt AI to act as a performance coach who believes growth occurs through planned, intentional acts of discomfort. Request AI to help you create a short, ten-day "discomfort ladder" with small, achievable challenges that gradually push your confidence and skills. Describe situations you usually avoid and outline the professional you aim to become. Complete one challenge at a time, briefly reflect on what you learned, and track your progress to see your comfort zone expand.

Move 12: Speak Up Without Burning Bridges

As you grow, you'll encounter times when discomfort comes not from taking action but from speaking out, especially when something feels wrong.

"It's really difficult to speak truth to power, but if you don't, you risk both your reputation and your work," said Deirdre Breakenridge, CEO of Pure Performance, a coaching and training company.

Breakenridge spent her career watching young professionals sit in meetings with a sinking feeling that something wasn't right. Data being stretched, promises that couldn't be kept, and a campaign that didn't align with the brand's values. "*Afterward, they tell me, I didn't want to seem difficult, or I was worried my question wouldn't be taken seriously.*"

Breakenridge doesn't shame them for that. She remembers feeling it herself, "the discomfort of a respectful question is almost always more bearable than the damage of staying silent." Her advice is to anchor your voice in care. "Instead of calling someone out, ask, '*Can we walk through the implications of this? Is there any risk we're not seeing?*'"

That's ethics in practice—not a showy display, but a consistent habit of safeguarding the work, the customer, and your own integrity.

Ask AI for Help: Prompt AI to act like an executive communication coach. Describe a situation where something feels off, but you're hesitant to speak up. Ask AI to help you clarify the actual risk of staying silent, distinguish facts from emotion, and reframe your concern into respectful, curiosity-driven language. Practice two or three professional phrases before the meeting, then use a simple self-check afterward to evaluate if you acted with integrity and composure.

Move 13: Build Credibility Through Value Tracking

Once you've found your voice, the next step is to showcase your value—because integrity is reinforced when your impact is evident.

John Skroly led agencies, enterprise teams, and major marketing organizations. But his biggest lesson for early-career marketers is: "Credibility isn't given; it's built through curiosity, clear thinking, and proof of impact."

Skroly started his career among Harvard MBAs and experienced the same intimidation many young marketers feel today. Instead of pretending he knew everything, he focused on what he *could* control: "Understand the product. Understand the customer. Start there."

At Pitney Bowes, a global commerce and shipping company trusted by thousands of businesses, Skroly followed the same approach. Instead of rushing into campaigns, he spent his first two to three months learning. He sat with product managers, reviewed workflows, and spoke directly with customers. His go-to opener was simple: "I'm new here...what does our product actually help you do?"

That honesty disarmed people and sparked real conversations. For you, the lesson is clear: Even in big, established companies, credibility starts with curiosity, not confidence. Understanding the product isn't optional—it's the foundation of every smart marketing decision you'll make.

But here's the part most young marketers sometimes overlook: Every idea, experiment, or recommendation you make communicates a value statement. Even if you're new, you're sending a signal about how you think—and leaders notice when you support your ideas with evidence.

John shares a painful story: "A brilliant marketing manager was let go because she couldn't demonstrate the value of her work... even though her campaigns generated $7.5M in revenue. Nobody knew because she didn't show that her work drove the business result." That's the trap marketers need to avoid. You're doing meaningful work, but if the value isn't visible, it might as well not matter.

> **Ask AI for Help:** Prompt AI to think like a revenue-focused marketing leader. Describe your current role, projects, and how success is measured on your team. Ask AI to assist in identifying where you're already delivering value and to create a simple weekly tracker that links your work to business results. Use it regularly, and practice summarizing your impact in one or two clear sentences so leaders can see the cause-and-effect of your contributions.

Move 14: Challenge Assumptions With Curiosity, Not Ego

With your value on the table, the next level of grit is to improve the thinking around you—not through ego, but through curiosity.

"It's easier to agree with a strategy than to ask the questions that make it better," Noted Nitin Kartik, CEO of Caribou Strategic. Early in his career, he noticed how quickly teams—especially junior marketers—default to agreement. Not because an idea is strong, but because silence feels safer than speaking up. Yet, as he explained, "I've had to learn when to challenge—not to win, but to help the team see blind spots."

That shift is the essence of intellectual grit: the willingness to slow down, identify the assumption everyone overlooks, and do so with humility rather than bravado. Nitin believes true growth rarely comes from easy projects. "You don't really grow from projects that go smoothly. The learning happens when things break, and you have to figure out why." That kind of learning only occurs when you're willing to ask uncomfortable questions: Why this approach? What evidence supports it? What risk aren't we talking about?

For early-career marketers, this isn't defiance. It's a service. Grit involves having the courage to challenge ideas to improve work, reduce risks, and make the team smarter. Sometimes, the person who asks the question no one else will is the most valuable person in the room.

> **Ask AI for Help:** Prompt AI to think like a senior strategist. Describe a project or decision where you feel uncertain but hesitant to question the direction. Ask AI to help you uncover the hidden assumptions behind the current plan and generate thoughtful, respectful questions that strengthen your thinking. Practice one humility-based opener before your next meeting, and use a simple weekly review to train yourself to notice assumptions before they lead to mistakes.

All of these habits come back into focus in Nala's email—the quiet moment when her true growth started. We follow her story one year afterward.

Epilogue: Nala Chooses the Harder Right

Twelve months after the "green arrows" email, Nala's title remained the same, but her reputation had improved.

She could now explain the campaign's performance in clear language, linking segments, channels, and results while being open about the weak spots. Before each leadership review, she prepared two brief lists: what was working and what was concerning her. She led with both.

At a meeting, a senior leader asked, "If we move more budget into this channel, what are we risking?" Nala didn't freeze. She reviewed the data, the assumptions they made, and a small test she would conduct before a full shift. She didn't promise certainty. She showed her thinking.

After the meeting, Matt, the VP of Sales, stopped her in the hallway. "When you first emailed me about those warning signs, I worried you'd slow us down," he admitted. "Now I know you're helping us see the truth faster. That's how we win."

Her slides were still the least flashy in the room, but they were the ones people shared and referenced most often.

When a friend complained that their company "didn't value integrity," Nala recalled Stockdale, Duckworth, Collins, and the leaders whose stories you've just read. She realized something simple yet important. The real gap wasn't between knowing what grit and integrity are and having a job that "appreciates" them; it was between hoping to be seen as trustworthy and choosing, day after day, to act as someone who is. That decision had already begun to change her career.

Works Cited

Cengage Group. (2023). Graduate employability report. Cengage Group.

Collins, J. (2001). Good to great: Why some companies make the leap ... and others don't. HarperBusiness.

Duckworth, A. (2016). Grit: The power of passion and perseverance. Scribner.

National Association of Colleges and Employers. (2025, January 13). The gap in perceptions of new grads' competency proficiency and resources to shrink it. NACE.

ZipRecruiter. (2023). College major regret survey. ZipRecruiter.

CHAPTER 4: RELATE & EMPATHIZE

"Between stimulus and response, there is a space.
In that space is our power to choose our response.
In our response lies our growth and our freedom."
—Viktor Frankl

Field Story: Before the Room Was Ready

Anthony had learned how to prepare.

He reviewed briefs before meetings. He rehearsed his talking points. He kept a running list of ideas in his notes app so he wouldn't freeze up when asked for input.

What he hadn't learned, at least not yet, was how to read the room.

Tension arose during a project kickoff with product, sales, and customer success teams. The goal was straightforward: to align on messaging for a new update to a healthcare platform. Within ten minutes, the conversation went off track.

The Product team needed precision. Sales required proof points. Customer success was concerned about the onboarding workload. Everyone spoke in brief bursts, each defending their own perspective.

Anthony listened, but only on the surface. In his head, he was busy preparing what to say.

When there was a pause, he jumped in. "I think the real opportunity here is differentiation," he said. "If we position this as a category shift rather than just an update, we can—"

He stopped mid-sentence.

No one responded. A few people looked at their screens. Someone coughed. The conversation went on without anyone engaging Anthony further.

After the meeting, Anthony replayed it in his mind. He hadn't said anything wrong. He'd actually said something smart. So why did it fall flat?

Later that afternoon, he ran into his manager, Priya, in the kitchen.

"How'd the kickoff feel?" Priya asked.

"Honestly? Weird," he said. "I felt invisible."

Priya nodded. "Let me ask you something. Before you spoke, how did you feel?"

Anthony hesitated. "Nervous. I didn't want to waste anyone's time."

"And how do you think everyone else was feeling?" she asked.

Anthony hadn't thought about that.

"Stressed?" he said. "Protective of their teams?"

"Exactly," Priya said. "You weren't wrong. You were just early. They needed to feel understood before they could hear ideas."

That night, Anthony kept thinking about her question—not what he said, but how he showed up. The next week, he tried a different approach.

In a follow-up meeting, he didn't rush to speak up. He observed his reactions: when he felt defensive or eager to jump in, he waited.

When sales raised concerns about adoption risk, Anthony spoke, but this time, differently.

"It sounds like you're worried this will create more friction for hospital administrators," he said. "Is that the main issue, or am I missing anything?"

The sales lead leaned back. "That's exactly it," she said. "We don't want to oversell."

The tone shifted. Product clarified the constraints. Customer success added context. Anthony didn't dominate the conversation; he was suddenly part of it.

Afterward, the product manager pulled him aside. "Thanks for slowing things down in there," she said. "That helped."

Anthony walked back to his desk with a quiet realization. Relating wasn't about saying more; it was about managing himself well enough to create space for others. That felt like a different kind of skill—one he didn't realize he needed to develop.

Remember this: being right doesn't mean you're heard. You can prepare well and offer a sharp insight, but it still might fall flat—not because the idea is wrong, but because the room isn't *ready* to receive it.

If that's happened to you, the issue was probably not intelligence. It was sequence.

Even Leaders Who See Reality Clearly Can Miss the Room

Mark Stouse spent decades as a corporate CMO before founding Proof Analytics, a causal AI platform. He's known for his directness and ability to cut through noise. When I asked him about emotional intelligence, he offered a confession, not advice.

When I started Proof, I told myself I wouldn't be like Don Quixote, meaning no tilting at windmills or crusading against a market that wasn't ready to listen. "I don't necessarily think I kept my promise to myself very well."

His early messaging, by his own description, was "really hardcore." The issue wasn't accuracy; what he said was true. The issue was that he hadn't studied the tribe. "I didn't really understand just how tribally cohesive marketing culture and the marketing belief systems are," he said. "Even though what I said was mostly accurate, it was very ill-considered because I lacked emotional intelligence for those people."

What made it more difficult? Using emotional intelligence to challenge the status quo can feel like betrayal. "Emotional intelligence in those circumstances feels like a sellout," Mark admitted. The discipline he's learned? "Part of emotional intelligence is knowing when not to say a damn thing, no matter what."

You Can Be Right and Still Lose

Ayse Guvencer did the right thing for the wrong reason — and paid for it with a relationship she couldn't rebuild.

Guvencer has over twenty years of experience in marketing, including senior roles at Google. When she saw her team being bullied by another director, she followed her instincts: she stepped in between the bully and her team, taking on the pressure herself for six months before a mentor finally advised her to report it to HR.

She did. And the situation escalated in ways she didn't anticipate.

That's when things unraveled. "When you do these kinds of things in corporate settings, you become the problem for HR — because HR's job, like any HR, is to protect the company." The formal inquiry escalated to a Senior VP who had been an ally. By the time it reached him, her relationship with him and her standing in the company were in ruins. When redundancies arrived, she accepted one.

What went wrong wasn't that she acted. It was how she framed it.

"I should have gone to the Senior VP first," she said. "And explained it not in terms of what this meant to me — but what it meant to the company. These are not our values. This behavior is reducing productivity. Deadlines are being missed. Teams can't function." The reframing matters: a personal grievance asks someone to take a side. A business case asks someone to protect what they already own.

The second mistake was the sequence. She escalated formally before she had secured her coalition. "You need allies," she said. "You need people in your corner before the conversation gets bigger than you."

Her advice for early-career marketers hits the main point: "Start building relationships intentionally from the very beginning — because you're going to need them long before you realize you do."

The lesson isn't about suppressing emotion or avoiding tough conversations. It's about timing, language, and the relationships you develop before the stakes get high. In corporate settings, even the most principled stance needs a coalition to endure.

Why Smart Graduates Struggle at Work

Anthony's experience wasn't a personal shortcoming. It was a pattern, and if you've felt it too, there's a reason that goes deeper than attitude or effort.

Many Gen Z professionals entered the workforce after COVID-19 disrupted the years when workplace instincts usually develop. Internships disappeared. Informal mentoring vanished. The casual, in-person moments where you observe how a senior colleague handles a difficult conversation, or how a team disagrees without breaking apart — those also disappeared.

What employers sometimes interpret as unpreparedness is often something more specific: a generation that learned the curriculum but missed the apprenticeship.

The data reflects both sides of that gap. Fewer than one in four recent graduates believe they have all the skills their roles require, and employers largely agree. HR leaders identify teamwork (55%) and business etiquette (50%) as the most common gaps among new hires, with professional communication close behind (Hult International Business School, 2023). Graduates are learning what to do. They're arriving without enough practice in working with others while doing it.

Employer behavior continues to reinforce the concern. A December 2023 survey by Intelligent.com revealed that 38% of employers avoid hiring recent college graduates, preferring older workers (Intelligent.com, 2023). Respondents pointed to weak communication, defensiveness toward feedback, difficulty managing workloads, and limited professionalism. Some organizations reported terminating recent graduates within their first year.

The demand for these skills isn't new, and it isn't going away. Analysis of U.S. job postings from 2010 to 2019 reveals that employers increasingly require soft skills like communication and people management, often alongside technical qualifications (Lyu & Liu, 2021). The same research highlights a persistent paradox: soft skills are requested more often, yet organizations struggle to measure or systematically develop them.

Deloitte's 2025 Human Capital Trends report highlights a growing experience gap as early-career professionals enter hybrid workplaces with fewer apprenticeship-style learning opportunities. Employers expect relational judgment, but the traditional pathways that once developed it—such as observation, modeling, and real-time correction—have weakened.

The research points to a clear conclusion: emotional intelligence is required across industries, expected in hiring, and seldom taught intentionally. Graduates feel unprepared. Employers feel frustrated. The skills most in demand are the least explicitly cultivated.

Emotional Intelligence Is a Set of Skills, Not a Personality Trait

The gap employers keep describing, the one that gets graduates passed over, talked about in performance reviews, and sometimes let go, almost always comes down to the same thing. Not technical skills. Not intelligence. How you manage yourself and your relationships when the pressure is real.

That's emotional intelligence, and despite how often the term gets thrown around, most people treat it as a personality type rather than what it actually is: four trainable skills. Self-awareness. Self-management. Social awareness. Relationship management (Goleman, 2020). Not fixed qualities. Behaviors you can build. Think of them as a ladder.

- First, notice what you're feeling.
- Second, regulate it.
- Third, read the room.
- Fourth, respond in a way that builds trust.

The sequence matters as much as the skills. Skip a rung, and people feel it.

That's what happened to Anthony at the start of this chapter. He tried to influence the room before managing his own anxiety. His voice became tense. His body language revealed uncertainty. He was presenting a strategy but transmitting stress. The team responded more to the signal than to the idea.

If you want to apply this tomorrow, try this sequence in your next meeting:

- **Name your internal state.** Before you speak, ask: What am I feeling right now—nervous, defensive, eager to impress?
- **Regulate before reacting.** Slow your breathing. Relax your shoulders. Lower your speaking pace.
- **Scan the room.** Who looks guarded? Who seems open? Who hasn't spoken?
- **Align your response.** Instead of pushing your point, ask a clarifying question. Invite others in.

Emotional intelligence is not about being soft. It's about being effective.

In the T-GROWTH framework, Relate and Empathize are at the core because credibility is built here. Ideas don't gain momentum solely through logic; they advance when people feel understood.

The encouraging part? All of this can be improved. With attention and feedback, you can deliberately develop these skills. Start small. Practice in low-risk settings. Then reflect afterward.

Awareness. Regulation. Observation. Alignment. That's the progression from intention to influence.

But there's a complication.

Why Emotional Intelligence Fails Under Pressure

Emotional intelligence often collapses when the stakes rise. The reason is neurological.

David Rock's SCARF model explains why (Rock, 2008). The brain continuously monitors five social domains for signs of threat: Status, Certainty, Autonomy, Relatedness, and Fairness. Each one represents something your brain treats as essential to survival in a social environment.

Status is your sense of where you stand relative to others in the room. *Certainty* is your ability to predict what comes next. *Autonomy* is your feeling of control over your own choices and actions. *Relatedness* is whether you feel trusted, included, and safe with the people around you. *Fairness* is whether you believe you're being treated equitably.

When any one of these domains feels threatened, your brain responds the same way it would to physical danger. Cortisol rises. Activity in the prefrontal cortex, the region responsible for self-regulation, empathy, and complex reasoning, drops.

Under threat, your best capacities go offline.

Anthony wasn't bad at meetings. His brain was in protection mode because his status felt uncertain. He lacked clarity about what was expected, and he had little control over how the discussion would unfold. He wasn't sure he belonged. Multiple SCARF domains were triggered at once, which affected his ability to think clearly.

This is why smart, prepared professionals say the wrong thing — or say nothing at all. It's not a character flaw. It's a threat response.

Here's the practical approach before you speak: scan for threats.

Ask yourself:

- Does my status feel challenged — am I worried about how I'm being perceived?

- Am I unclear about what's expected of me in this situation?
- Do I feel excluded, dismissed, or like I don't belong here?

Name the trigger. Slow your breathing. Lower your speaking pace. Even small physiological regulation can restore cognitive control and bring your prefrontal cortex back online.

If threat shuts down emotional intelligence, then the next question is obvious: what lowers threat? The answer is psychological safety.

Why Psychological Safety Builds Better Work

Harvard professor Amy Edmondson defines psychological safety as a shared belief that a team is safe for interpersonal risk-taking (Edmondson, 2018). It means people can ask questions, admit mistakes, disagree respectfully, and offer incomplete ideas without fear of embarrassment or punishment.

This is not about comfort. It is about reducing social threat.

Edmondson's research found something counterintuitive: high-performing teams report more errors, not fewer. They surface issues earlier. They challenge assumptions sooner. They correct faster. The difference is not talent—it is safety.

When psychological safety is high, SCARF threats are lower. Status feels more stable. Fairness is more visible. Relatedness is reinforced. The prefrontal cortex remains active. Curiosity and regulation stay accessible.

When safety is low, the opposite happens. Meetings become performances. People hedge their language. They protect their image. Emotional intelligence shifts from connection to self-preservation.

For early-career marketers, this is crucial.

You may have strong emotional intelligence skills and still struggle in a low-safety environment. That does not automatically mean you lack maturity. It may mean the system is operating in threat mode.

So what can you do without formal authority?

Start small:

- Admit micro-mistakes publicly.
- Credit others quickly and specifically.
- Ask questions that clarify rather than threaten status.
- Invite quieter voices into the discussion.

These behaviors lower threat and increase relatedness. They create pockets of safety.

Psychological safety is not a soft skill. It is an operating condition. When that condition exists, emotional intelligence becomes usable rather than theoretical.

The Skills Behind Trust and Influence

The three frameworks connect:

- Goleman's model defines emotional intelligence as the skills that help you manage yourself and relate to others.
- Rock's SCARF model explains *why* those skills fail under pressure—the neuroscience of the threat response that shuts down your best capacities.
- Edmondson's psychological safety research explains *when* emotional intelligence practice becomes possible—the environmental conditions that keep threat responses low and preserve prefrontal function.

For early-career marketers, these points have practical implications. First, concentrate on self-awareness and self-management before trying to influence relationships. Second, learn to recognize SCARF threats—both in yourself and in the environment—so you can identify what's happening and manage your response. Third, seek out or help establish pockets of psychological safety where authentic practice is encouraged.

The good news is consistent across all three research streams: these are not fixed traits. Emotional intelligence is learnable. Threat responses can be managed with specific techniques. Psychological safety can be established, even by those without formal authority. The behaviors are acts of discipline.

Advice from Leaders Who Build Trust Across Teams

Move 15: Relationships Compound Over Time

"People underestimate how much their success depends on relationships," said Reid Kiser, managing partner at Kiser Healthcare Solutions. "You can be great at your job, but if you can't work well with others, it will catch up with you eventually."

Kiser explained that emotional intelligence isn't just a soft skill—it's a boost for your career. "You end up working with the same people again and again, sometimes years later. If you burn bridges or act like you know it all, people remember. They don't forget."

He shared that early-career professionals often focus on proving competence, but what truly earns trust is relational awareness. "The people who advance fastest aren't the smartest in the room. They're the ones who know how to collaborate, listen, and adapt to different personalities," Kiser said. "They make it easier for others to work with them."

In his experience, strong marketers take the time to understand how others operate before proposing ideas. "You have to read the room. Every team has its own dynamics, pressures, and unspoken rules. If you ignore them and come in hot with solutions, you create resistance rather than momentum."

Early-career marketers often believe that performance speaks for itself. However, without empathy, their performance may hinder influence. "Relationships are cumulative," Kiser said. "Every interaction either deposits trust or withdraws from it. Over time, that balance determines who is invited into real conversations and who isn't."

The core message is uncomfortable: how you make people feel is just as important as what you provide. When you listen, stay curious, and view relationships as long-term investments, doors open quietly—and remain open.

> **Ask AI for Help:** Prompt AI to act as an executive coach who specializes in emotional intelligence. Describe a recent interaction where you sensed tension or a missed connection. Request AI to reflect on what likely occurred, identify the emotions that may have influenced the exchange, and suggest one small change to improve how others experience working with you. Try that change in your next interaction and evaluate whether you deposited or withdrew trust this week.

Move 16: Your Idea Flopped. That's Data, Not Defeat

The feedback didn't come from a consultant or a senior VP. It came from a patient.

Geoffrey Roche, senior vice president of Healthcare Solutions at Risepoint, had helped lead a bold repositioning campaign for a regional healthcare system. New physicians, new services, new CEO, the campaign was called *Meet the New Face of Healthcare.* Leadership approved it. The agency believed in it. The energy in the room was high.

Then a member of their patient family advisory council stopped everything. She told them she didn't understand how they could claim to be the new face of healthcare when every time she came to their emergency room, she waited hours to be admitted.

"We thought we were being audacious," Geoffrey reflected. "And the feedback was pretty direct that it wasn't landing the way we thought it would."

His CEO, a former nurse who had privately questioned the campaign's boldness from the start, used the moment to shift the conversation. Her instinct had been right. The team had outvoted her with collective enthusiasm. The lesson she learned wasn't about the campaign itself; it was about whose voice had been missing from the room.

What followed was a genuine reset. The team went back out and listened to patients, clinicians, and employers. A year and a half later, they launched a new access initiative, leading with transparency instead of aspiration. They acknowledged publicly that their emergency room had work to do. Patient experience improved. The redirected care went where it should have gone.

For a Gen Z marketer, the instinct in that moment is familiar: you worked hard on something, you believed in it, and someone told you it wasn't working. The pull toward defending your work is almost automatic. Self-management isn't about suppressing that instinct. It's about creating enough space between the feedback and your response so that new information can actually reach you.

Geoffrey's team didn't fail because they were wrong. They struggled because they were too invested in being right. The correction came when they let a patient tell them the truth and listened.

Ask AI for Help: Prompt AI to act like an executive performance coach. Describe a moment when feedback caused frustration or defensiveness. Ask AI to help identify the emotion behind your reaction, separate the feedback from the story you told yourself about it, and reframe the input as useful data. Practice a grounding phrase before your next review, and afterward, check if you focused on learning rather than pride.

Move 17: Read the Vibe, Not Just the Words

Kaitlyn O'Connor, the co-founder of Elevare Law, knows the exact moment when someone truly understands her. "When I read the deliverable, I think that is exactly what we talked about. This is perfect. Send it out." She also knows the moment when they don't.

Her firm had just announced its biggest reveal ever: four new partner-level attorneys joining a nine-member practice. The marketing director met with the team, asked some initial questions, and developed a clear plan — including an initial step of meeting with the managing partner before speaking with anyone else. She skipped it, went directly to the other partners, gathered what she thought was necessary, and created content that Kaitlyn described as not reflecting "at all what our firm does or who our audience is." Kaitlyn then spent two days rewriting everything herself.

"There weren't many follow-up or clarifying questions," she said. "We assumed we were all on the same page." They heard her, but they just didn't understand her.

This is the gap that social awareness aims to fill. In Goleman's model, social awareness involves accurately reading others — detecting not just their words but the underlying meaning, context, and what isn't being said. O'Connor's standard makes this clear: if you can accurately reflect back what someone said, you've shown understanding. If you can't, you were listening to respond, not to understand.

The solution is easier than it seems. "I will be 100 percent more confident in someone if they tell me when they don't understand something," she said. Admitting uncertainty isn't a weakness in this situation — it's evidence that you're trying to understand clearly rather than making assumptions. And for a client moving quickly through a high-stakes announcement, that honesty is more valuable than confidently executing the wrong brief.

Her baseline expectation isn't complicated: "Ongoing communication and check-ins, being upfront and transparent about what you know, what you don't know, and what you need to learn."

Social awareness isn't mind-reading. It's verifying that what you think you heard matches what was actually intended before you build anything on top of it.

> **Ask AI for Help:** Prompt AI to act like an executive communication coach. Describe a recent conversation where you received feedback or direction. Ask AI to help you reflect on what was said, what was implied, and where you may have assumed rather than confirmed. Practice using one alignment-check phrase in your next meeting and observe whether your accuracy improves.

Move 18: Win-Wins Start with Listening, Not Directing

Mike Slusarz, managing partner of Healthcare at Princeton Partners, describes what trust looks like when someone is scared. "You can see their dilated pupils, rapid breathing, and muscle tension."

He had asked a young marketer to take on a website initiative—work new to both of them. Her response was immediate.

"Oh my God, I can't do that. I can't do that. There's no way I can do it."

Most managers would hear that as a no. Slusarz heard something different.

"I could just see it in her face. I could see it in her eyes," he said. "She wanted this. She saw it as a great opportunity, but her words said I can't."

Slusarz detected her desire to take on responsibility, masked in her words.

So, he didn't pull the assignment back. He reframed what was at stake.

"Don't worry about it," he told her. "I'm on a learning curve too. We'll learn together as we go through this."

By admitting his uncertainty, Slusarz reframed failure. This wasn't a test she could fail; it was an experiment they ran together. The psychological safety he established allowed her to say yes.

As the project advanced, trust was built through consistent communication. "She was a great communicator with me," Slusarz said. "She gave me updates, told me where she was, and always asked thoughtful questions."

"Strong relationship management involves authenticity, transparency, and good communication," Slusarz said, describing what "If you can show passion for your idea, and for their thoughts as well, and blend them, you get the win-win."

The lesson is subtle but significant. Slusarz didn't push the marketer toward growth. He listened intently enough to understand what she truly wanted, created a safe environment for her to try, and then stepped back so she could become someone she didn't yet realize she could be.

That's the win-win: not just a successful project.

> **Ask AI for Help:** Prompt AI to act like a leader who builds trust by listening first, then guiding second. Describe a situation where you felt the urge to direct or take control. Ask AI to help you identify what the other person may have needed at that moment and where you could have created more psychological safety. Practice one listening-first response next time and reflect on whether you built shared ownership or simply solved the problem yourself.

Epilogue: Anthony Learns to Read the Room

Same cross-functional meeting. Same team: product, sales, customer success. Same goal: align on messaging for the upcoming platform release. And within ten minutes, the same drift sideways.

The product team aimed to emphasize technical specs. Sales emphasized customer proof points. Customer success warned about support ticket volume from the last launch.

Anthony felt the old impulse rise, the urge to cut through the noise with a sharp strategic take. He had one ready. It was solid.

He didn't say it.

Instead, he realized what was happening to him. His heartbeat sped up. His jaw clenched. He recognized the pattern: feeling threatened by status. He wanted to prove he was worthy of being in this room.

He took a breath and asked himself Priya's question: *How is everyone else feeling right now?*

He watched as the product lead's arms were crossed, while the sales director kept glancing at her phone. Customer success hadn't made eye contact with anyone in five minutes. The room wasn't ready for ideas; it was stuck in defensive mode.

So Anthony did something he wouldn't have done two months earlier.

"Can I ask a question?" he said. "It feels like we're each protecting something important. What's the thing we're most afraid of getting wrong this time?"

Silence. Then the sales director put her phone down.

"Honestly? I'm afraid we'll overpromise again, and I'll spend Q3 apologizing to customers."

Product uncrossed their arms. "And I'm afraid we'll water down the messaging so much that no one will understand what's actually new."

Customer success finally looked up. "I just don't want to be the last to hear about any changes."

The tension didn't go away, but it shifted. What was once defensive became diagnostic. They weren't debating positions anymore—they were voicing their fears. Once the fears became visible, they could address them.

Anthony's strategic idea? He presented it twenty minutes later, after the room had actually listened to one another. This time, it resonated.

After the meeting, Priya caught him in the hallway.

"That question you asked," she said. "Where did it come from?"

Anthony thought about it. "I realized I was about to do the same thing I did last time—say something smart at the wrong moment. So, I asked myself what the room needs rather than what I want to contribute."

Priya smiled. "That's the whole game, you know. Most people never figure it out."

Anthony nodded. He didn't feel like a different person. He was still nervous. He still wanted to be seen as smart. The difference was that he had learned to notice those impulses before they took over his actions—and to choose a different response.

The room hadn't gotten any less difficult. He'd just learned how to meet it.

Works Cited

Deloitte. (2025). 2025 Global Human Capital Trends: Closing the experience gap. Deloitte Insights.

Edmondson, A. C. (2018). The fearless organization. Wiley.

Goleman, D. (2020). Emotional intelligence: Why it can matter more than IQ (25th anniversary ed.). Bantam.

Hult International Business School. (2023). The global Gen Z and the future of work report 2023. Hult International Business School.

Intelligent.com. (2023, December 12). Nearly 4 in 10 employers avoid hiring recent college graduates in favor of older workers. Intelligent.com.

Lyu, W., & Liu, J. (2021). Soft skills, hard skills: What matters most? Evidence from job postings. Applied Energy, 300, 117307.

Rock, D. (2008). SCARF: A brain-based model for collaborating with and influencing others. NeuroLeadership Journal, 1, 44-52.

CHAPTER 5: OBSERVE & COMMUNICATE

"The audience does not need to tune themselves to you—
you need to tune your message to them."
—Nancy Duarte

Field Story: The Meeting Before the Meeting

Both Nala's and Mia's phones chimed simultaneously. They had 15 minutes until the marketing campaign budget approval meeting with the executive team.

Three weeks earlier, Nala and Mia had a similar meeting, which ended without a decision.

Last time, they entered the budget meeting with twelve slides of campaign data, clear charts, and a recommendation they believed was solid. The flagship campaign looked costly and overrated. Other, less celebrated efforts seemed to be doing more real work. To Nala, the logic was clear.

After the presentation, the CEO thanked them for being thorough. The VP of sales said he'd "need to think about it." Nala returned to her desk and stared at the slide deck. She had done what she thought good marketers were supposed to do. She had shown the work. She had backed up every claim. She had tried to anticipate every objection.

Mia rolled her chair closer to Nala and asked, "Our presentation was solid. Why do you think the exec team ghosted us?"

That question stayed with them, so they started over with a different one: *What does leadership already believe about our campaigns, and why?*

The answer came quickly. Throughout the company, one phrase kept recurring: the flagship campaign drives pipeline. People repeated it in meetings as if it were a proven fact. Over time, the repetition made it feel true.

Nala decided to test it more rigorously. If the company was about to commit more money based on that assumption, she wanted more than a familiar dashboard. She asked a data science consultant to help examine the relationship more carefully. The results were surprising.

Yes, the flagship campaign was associated with pipeline activity. But once other variables were taken into account, the causal link weakened. Another pattern stood out more clearly: sales-enablement content such as case studies, demo videos, and one-page briefs had a stronger effect on decision-making.

The enablement tools have a smaller budget but cause more closed deals than the flagship campaign. Nala felt the satisfaction of finding something real, followed by a more troubling thought: *What if we're right again and nobody moves again?*

Mia's instinct was to defer to Nala for the numbers, but Mia could spot patterns in people. Mia asked, "Who has to let go of an old story if this is true?"

That question changed the work.

Together, they mapped the room before the meeting. The CEO wanted clarity, not a lecture. The VP of sales had repeated the flagship story for the past year and would need a way to shift without looking foolish. The CFO might be open to reallocating budget, but only if the case felt credible and practical.

Nala asked the CFO for a short meeting before the budget review. Nala didn't go in trying to persuade the CFO. She went in trying to understand what the CFO needed.

That conversation changed everything.

The CFO was not defending the old allocation. She was waiting for someone to challenge it in a grounded, clear, and business-impact-driven way. Her problem was not resistance. It was confidence.

When Nala told Mia, Mia smiled. "So, the issue isn't the data. It's orientation."

Then Mia cut the deck from twelve slides to one. Nala looked at her in disbelief. "One slide?"

"Last time, we showed all the work," Mia said. "This time, we show what the work means."

On the morning of the next meeting, the CEO opened with a blunt summary. "We're here to decide where the marketing budget goes."

The VP of sales spoke first. "The pipeline's been uneven, but the flagship campaign has always driven interest. We've seen that before."

The CFO leaned back in her chair. "Interest is not the same as movement."

Nala felt the old urge rise in her chest. Explain everything. Walk them through the analysis. Defend every assumption. Prove she had done the work. Instead, Nala began where they had agreed to start.

"We've funded the flagship campaign because it has been linked to pipeline activity for the past six quarters," she said. "That belief is understandable. It shaped how we've budgeted."

A few heads nodded.

Then she moved to the tension.

"But when we tested that assumption more carefully, the story changed. The flagship still correlates with the pipeline. However, it is not the strongest driver of decision-making. Late-stage enablement content has a stronger causal effect, and we've underinvested in it."

The room got quieter. The VP of sales looked up. "That tracks with what reps actually use in closing conversations."

The CFO asked, "What happens if we shift the budget?"

Nala answered without reaching for another slide. "We lower the risk of overinvesting in visibility that creates attention but not action. We put more money into the tools buyers use when they are deciding. If the pattern holds, we should see faster movement in active deals within ninety days."

The CEO looked around the table, then nodded. "Approved."

Mia looked at Nala and gave her a slight smile. "That landed."

Nala nodded. Same company. Same budget. Same people. Different result. Not because the data changed. Because the room did.

Learning to See Before Speaking

What Nala and Mia figured out in one high-stakes meeting, Stephen Zakur has spent a career refining into a discipline. As co-founder and CEO of ThinkStream.ai and a longtime founder-advisor to startups and enterprises, Stephen Zakur has seen what happens when smart teams confuse activity with understanding.

"Marketing always comes down to storytelling," Zakur said, "but not the kind most people think of. The best marketing helps people see clearly so they can make decisions."

Early in his career, Zakur depended too much on education and confidence. "I had ample formal training," he admitted, "but tenured colleagues had domain experience. I wasn't humble enough to recognize what I didn't know." The result was friction. Ideas didn't land because the room wasn't yet aligned.

Over time, Zakur changed his approach. Before making his case, he learned to identify the story the room was already telling itself, the assumptions people had formed before he said a word. "When you walk into a meeting," he said, "everyone already has a story in their heads about you and why you're there." His job became interrupting that story with something precise enough to stop it.

In one case, he helped a founder clarify an AI product; the breakthrough wasn't a list of features or a chart. A single reframing challenged a common assumption, creating space for a new story. "It's rarely just facts and figures that drive decisions," Zakur said. "People need a story where they can say, 'Oh, I get it.'"

That discipline—observe first, orient the room, then speak—became his advantage. Not louder opinions or better slides. Just the ability to translate complexity into shared understanding, enabling decisions to finally move forward.

Why Communication Breaks Down at Work

Employers prioritize one key skill in early-career marketers: communication. However, it's also the skill they're most often disappointed in.

Hickman and Stoica (2023) found that written and oral communication are the primary sources of dissatisfaction among new hires, even among those with strong analytical or technical skills. The issue isn't whether young marketers can analyze data, but whether they can explain what that data means for the business.

Mercado and Mercado (2025) compared employers' ratings of the importance of communication skills with recent graduates' self-assessments of their proficiency. Employers rated it 4.69 out of 5, while graduates rated themselves 3.67. The biggest differences weren't in grammar or formatting but in persuasion, storytelling, and message clarity.

That distinction is important. Academic training teaches you to write essays and reports. Work requires you to persuade others to make decisions.

The Association of American Colleges & Universities (AAC&U, 2018) identified a clear gap between the importance of workplace writing and graduates' readiness: 76% of business executives and 78% of hiring managers consider written communication very important, but only 33% of executives and 45% of hiring managers believe recent graduates are well prepared to communicate effectively in the workplace.

In February 2021, Kovács and Vámosi Zarandné analyzed 5,548 digital marketing job ads posted over one month and found a clear message for entry-level candidates: knowing the tools isn't enough. While hard skills are essential, employers often emphasize soft skills, especially communication and teamwork, since someone needs to turn observations into actions. Practical takeaway: when you share results, include a "so what / now what" line that suggests the next step for busy decision-makers (Kovács & Vámosi Zarandné, 2022).

Even when companies attempt to share insights using tools, communication issues still arise. In a 2021 survey by Exasol, a data analytics software company, of 500 executives and data professionals, 82% said they regularly use dashboards to share insights, yet 53% mentioned that dashboards are often ignored because they're difficult to interpret. The main reasons include: inadequate context (61%), information overload (54%), and lack of customization (46%) (Exasol, 2021).

The research highlights a specific failure: Graduates can gather and analyze information, but they struggle to turn that analysis into shared understanding. They write to inform rather than to guide. They present data without context. They describe situations without clarifying what is needed.

To understand why observation and communication break down so often, it helps to look at two models from outside marketing. One explains how people make sense of what they see. The other explains how they turn that sensemaking into action.

The Missing Step Between Data and Decisions

Many junior marketers go straight from observing to acting. They present data and suggest actions, skipping the most important step: orientation.

Senior executives repeatedly observed that early-career marketers often present data without relevant context for the specific situation. However, orientation is where credibility is built. It's where marketers show they understand how executives think, assess risk, and make decisions.

In the opening scene, the shift occurred when the room was given context to use. The executives were not asked to admire the analysis. They were given a clearer basis for judgment. The behavior comes from one of the most pressure-tested environments imaginable: a fighter cockpit at 30,000 feet.

The OODA Loop was created by Colonel John Boyd, a U.S. Air Force fighter pilot and strategist who studied why some teams consistently outmaneuver others in uncertain situations (Coram, 2002). Boyd established the framework for adversarial situations—air combat and military strategy—where the aim was to act faster than an opponent. In business, this translates to something counterintuitive: winning teams don't just act faster, they understand the room more clearly before they do anything at all.

The four stages of the OODA Loop, applied to marketing

Observe. *You have the data. So does everyone else.* This is your raw intake, such as dashboards, campaign metrics, customer behavior, sales team feedback, and market signals. Most marketers are well-trained here, but observation is not enough.

Orient. *Nobody got promoted for stating the obvious. Context is literally the whole job.* This is where raw data becomes professional judgment. Orientation asks you to integrate what you're seeing with what it means, given your company's history, your audience's behavior, your executive team's risk tolerance, and the specific moment you're operating in. It's the stage where credibility is built. Senior leaders aren't looking for someone to read them a report. They're looking for someone who can tell them what the report means for the decisions they're already trying to make.

Decide. *If you have to convince the room, you've already lost it before you start.* A well-constructed orientation makes the decision almost self-evident. The debate shortens. Confidence rises. The recommendation no longer needs to be sold. It needs to be confirmed. That shift in the room is not accidental. It is the result of preparation.

Act. *Stop waiting for permission to move. Clarity is the green light.* Once shared understanding is clear, action happens naturally. Resources shift. Messaging updates. Priorities become sharper. The speed of execution is a natural result of good initial alignment.

How to Turn Insight into Shared Understanding

OODA is a thinking tool. It helps you understand complex information and develop a clear perspective. However, it doesn't show you how to communicate that perspective so others can act on it.

This is where many early-career marketers stall. The orientation is done. The analysis is sound. But the recommendation lands flat — acknowledged, tabled, or quietly set aside. For Nala and Mia, the room moved on because the communication didn't give the audience a clear path to act on it.

A second discipline becomes important here: a straightforward framework that converts private sensemaking into shared understanding.

In the 1970s, Barbara Minto was one of the first women hired as a consultant at McKinsey & Company, and she quickly recognized the same problem Boyd identified in the cockpit: under pressure, people process information poorly when it isn't structured for decision-making. Her solution was the Pyramid Principle, which led to what practitioners now call the SCR Framework: a method for communicating with busy executives who need context fast and clarity immediately (Management Consulted,

2025). The core idea was straightforward: lead with the answer, then provide the minimum context needed to support it. A clear method to do this is Situation → Complication → Resolution (SCR):

Situation: Begin with what everyone already agrees is true. Keep it brief — one or two sentences. The goal isn't to teach, but to confirm the shared understanding you're building on.

Complication: Introduce the tension. What has changed? What is no longer working? What risk is increasing? This is where your orientation appears. You're not just relaying facts — you're explaining why the current assumption is incomplete and why a decision is now necessary.

Resolution: Present a clear path forward. Be specific: offer a recommendation along with a way to test it. If you thoroughly addressed the situation and complication, your resolution should seem almost inevitable because you helped them understand the problem clearly.

Why Structure Earns the Right to Be Heard

As stated earlier, the written communication gap identified by the Association of American Colleges and Universities isn't about grammar or formatting. It's about structure. Recent graduates write to inform rather than to guide. They describe situations without explaining what those situations need.

SCR provides a process and guides the writer to answer three questions in sequence: What does my audience already believe? Why is that belief incomplete or wrong? What should they do about it?

Most early-career marketers skip the second question. They jump from data to a recommendation without earning the right to be heard. The complication is where that right is earned.

Where Good Thinking Turns Into Clear Communication

You've done the analysis. You know what the data means. You're thirty seconds from speaking in a meeting room or from hitting send on a recommendation. This is the moment most early-career marketers lose because their communication doesn't give the audience a clear path to act on it.

The intersection between OODA and SCR happens right here: after you've determined what's true, but before you speak.

That gap is where the Exasol finding becomes relevant. When 53% of executives say dashboards are regularly ignored because they're difficult to interpret, the problem isn't the data; it's the absence of a complication. There's no tension, no "why now," no reason the audience should care what the numbers say. SCR fixes that. It gives your thinking a shape leaders can move through quickly: context, tension, direction.

When both frameworks operate together:

What you figure out through OODA	What to communicate through SCR	Example in a marketing meeting
Observe: Notice what is happening without rushing to judgment.	**Situation**: State the current reality clearly and simply.	"Pipeline volume is up, but late-stage conversion has slowed for two quarters."
Orient: Interpret what matters, what has changed, and what may be causing the problem.	**Complication**: Explain the tension, risk, or mismatch the team needs to understand.	"We assumed awareness was the issue, but the slowdown appears later, when buyers are trying to reduce risk and make a decision."
Decide: Identify the most important conclusion or choice.	**Resolution**: State the recommendation or path forward.	"We should shift budget toward late-stage enablement content and test whether deal velocity improves over the next 90 days."
Act: Turn the decision into a next step that can be tested, measured, or implemented.	**Resolution, continued**: Clarify what happens next and how success will be judged.	"Reallocate 15% of campaign spend, monitor late-stage conversion, and review results at the next quarterly business review."

Observe what the orient/complication row accomplishes. From a CFO's point of view, that one sentence, *"we assumed awareness was the issue,"* marks the point where the conversation shifts from a simple update to a strategic challenge worth addressing. It reframes the data the executive already saw and clarifies why the current approach no longer applies. Without it, the solution is just a budget request. With it, the solution becomes a logical response to a known risk.

That's the core principle of this section: your orientation must be as precise as your complication. The complication is the "why now" and "why this" that give your recommendation its credibility.

Skip it, and your resolution lacks momentum. You're asking people to change direction without showing that the current path no longer works. That's the difference between informing and guiding — and closing that gap is one of the fastest ways for an early-career marketer to build a reputation for executive-level thinking.

Why Good Recommendations Still Get Rejected

A good recommendation can still fail if the marketer doesn't help others understand the situation before suggesting a solution. The work isn't just in the analysis; it's in the sequence. Get the sequence wrong, and the room argues with your conclusion instead of acting on it. That is a missed opportunity to be taken seriously the next time.

Consider Olivia Baker, a marketing manager at a B2B software company, who uses OODA and SCR thinking and reporting in her work. She represents a common scenario: being asked to explain why marketing-qualified leads aren't converting into sales-qualified leads at the expected rate. Leadership has already formed an opinion: the leads aren't good enough. Olivia has done the research. She sees a different story, and she knows that walking in with a contradictory conclusion, without proper support, will get her dismissed before she finishes her second slide.

Here's the thinking she did before she entered the room.

Observe (What changed)

- **Outcome:** MQL-to-SQL conversion fell from **18% to 11%** over two quarters.
- **Input:** Lead volume increased **25%**.
- **Process:** Time-to-first-contact rose from **4 hours to 22 hours**.
- **Organizational shift:** A new **sales development rep (SDR)** team was onboarded in Q2 using different call scripts. Sales says leads "aren't ready to talk."

Orient (What does the change mean?)

Baker believes leadership is focused on the wrong cause. Her hypothesis is that lead quality has remained stable, but the speed of follow-up has declined. As response times increased, more leads went cold before SDRs could reach them.

Supporting evidence:

- Leads contacted within **6 hours** convert at **23%.**
- Leads contacted after **12 hours** convert at only **8%.**
- The **scoring model has not changed**, but the **follow-up system has.**

Decide (What conclusion deserves attention?)

The drop in conversion is more likely due to a response-time issue than to lead quality.

Act (What should Baker recommend?)

Establish a **4-hour SLA** for high-scoring leads, with automated alerts and routing to experienced reps during ramp periods.

Why OODA depends on SCR to Shift Beliefs

Baker has done the hard part before the meeting starts. She separated what changed from what it might mean. She identified the belief the room is currently holding — and the evidence that challenges it. But insight alone won't shift that belief. Now she has to bring the room to the same conclusion she reached, in the time it takes leadership to decide whether to keep listening.

That requires a different tool. OODA told her what was true. SCR will determine whether anyone else acts on it.

Situation: MQL volume is up, but MQL → SQL conversion is down.

Complication: The scoring model didn't change. Speed-to-contact did. Conversion drops sharply after 6–12 hours.

Resolution: Set a 4-hour SLA for top-scoring leads, trigger automated alerts, and route hot leads to tenured reps during SDR ramp.

That's the pivot: she makes her orientation visible, so the recommendation feels logical rather than arguable.

The reason this works isn't just the recommendation itself, but what comes before it. By identifying the complication before suggesting a solution, Baker makes her perspective clear. The room doesn't see the resolution as an argument to judge; they see it as a logical response to a problem they now understand. That difference marks the line between a marketer who simply presents and a marketer who leads.

Why the Sequence Matters

Baker did not start with her recommendation. If she had opened with "We need a four-hour SLA," the VP of sales would have asked why, and she would have spent the meeting defending a conclusion rather than clarifying the problem. She would have lost the room before she had it.

Instead, she surfaced the belief she was challenging — that lead quality had declined — and dismantled it with her own data before the room could attach to it. She kept the situation brief, named the real complication, and proposed a solution that could be tested. That made the recommendation feel grounded rather than speculative.

OODA leads you to insight. SCR brings that insight into the room. Use your orientation to help others see what they have not yet seen.

How to Know if the SCR Works

Communication isn't complete when you stop talking. It's complete when others act on what you said or when you learn why they didn't. That means the SCR doesn't end when you finish presenting. It continues in the questions that follow, the decisions that result, and the feedback that surfaces when neither happens.

Watch for three signals.

Signal 1: The room engages with your frame, not just your data. Pay attention to where the follow-up questions land. If they focus on the complication (*"How confident are we that speed is the real issue?"*), you've successfully shifted the conversation. The audience is reasoning inside your interpretation. If the questions return to the situation *("Can you walk us through the numbers again?"*), your complication didn't land. The room is still looking for the story you were supposed to give them.

Signal 2: Others repeat your interpretation. The real test of a well-constructed SCR isn't whether the room nodded. It's whether the insight travels. If the CEO later tells another team, "Marketing found that our lead-decay problem is actually a speed-to-contact issue," your framing has become the shared language of the organization. That's the goal. An SCR that is repeated without your name attached has done its job completely.

Signal 3: The decision is final, or the reason it isn't becomes visible. Sometimes the SCR lands, but the decision doesn't follow. That gap is information, not failure. The resolution may need a smaller initial step to build confidence before a full commitment. There may be a budget constraint that wasn't visible in the room. Or the hesitation may be political, meaning someone with influence has a stake in the current direction that your data alone won't move. Recognizing a political constraint early doesn't mean your SCR was wrong. It means your next move needs to address the relationship, not just the argument.

If your SCR didn't produce the response you expected, work backward through three questions before you revise the recommendation itself:

- Did I establish shared ground, or did I assume it?
- Did my complication challenge the right belief?
- Did my resolution offer a clear and testable path forward?

Most of the time, a recommendation fails in the room because either the situation was too drawn out, the resolution was too vague, or the complication identified the wrong tension. Return there first.

Building Executive Briefing Skills

Understanding OODA and SCR is the first step. Using them consistently requires repetition.

Start small. Before your next team meeting or status update, write a two-sentence overview of the situation and a one-sentence description of the complication, even if you don't present them formally. Structuring your thoughts will sharpen your message.

Practice low-stakes communication. Use SCR in an email to your manager to summarize a project update. Use it in a Slack message to explain why a deadline shifted. The structure works at any scale, and the more you use it in routine moments, the more natural it will feel when the stakes are higher.

Seek feedback after sharing your message. Following a presentation or important discussion, ask a trusted colleague, "Did my main point come through? What question did it leave you with?" This closes the feedback loop and helps you determine whether your SCR was effective and where to improve next time.

Record yourself. Practice delivering an SCR out loud, then listen to it again. You'll notice where you're rushing through the complication or overloading the situation. Most people need fewer words than they think.

Use the AI prompts in this chapter. They're designed to help you organize real-world situations, not hypothetical ones. Bring an actual project, presentation, or decision you need to communicate, and work through the steps.

Move 19: Start with the Problem, Not the Solution

David Sylvan, a healthcare Chief Strategy, Innovation & Marketing Officer, believes marketers should get closer to the world they serve before they recommend what to do. As he put it, "I think marketing professionals need to be receptive to embedding themselves in the domains … that they are looking to serve holistically."

That belief stemmed from direct experience. When Sylvan helped establish an innovation function within a large health system, he noticed a pattern that hampered progress: teams were rushing to solutions before properly identifying the real need. In his words, "the starting with the solution seemed to be the ethos of the organization."

That habit caused waste. Ideas were scattered across "disparate pockets," with no consistent process for intake, evaluation, or enablement. People were building what Sylvan called "bridges to nowhere" because they had not done the insight work needed to understand the magnitude of the unmet need.

So he changed the rule: "We never want to see a solution. Bring us your problems."

> **Ask AI for Help:** Think like a strategy coach using the Socratic method. I'm going to paste a project, campaign idea, or recommendation I'm working on. Before discussing solutions, ask me five questions that test whether I've observed the situation closely enough, spoken to the right people, and separated symptoms from root causes. Then help me write three things: (1) the real problem, (2) the assumption that may be misleading the team, and (3) one small next step to test before scaling a solution.

Move 20: Make the Story Portable

Sean Malony, a senior marketing executive and go-to-market strategist in health and technology, judges clarity with a simple test: "If I leave the room, can someone else tell the story the same way I would?"

After leading product launches, acquisitions, and growth initiatives at startups and Fortune 50 companies, Malony learned that alignment doesn't come from better slides. It comes from story structure. "You don't have to give somebody a script," he said. "The story is already organized in their heads."

Malony bases communication on concrete examples—real customer or stakeholder situations that highlight the problem. Only after that does he introduce data, strategy, or recommendations. "Start with a real story," he explained. "That's what people remember."

When ideas don't land, he doesn't push harder; he listens. "If people aren't aligned," he said, "it usually means we haven't explained it clearly enough." For Malony, repetition isn't redundancy; it's how shared understanding across functions is built. The sign that clarity has been achieved is hearing others explain the idea later, accurately, in their own words. That's when communication stops being tied to a single messenger and becomes a shared resource for the business.

> **Ask AI for Help:** Prompt AI to think like a senior go-to-market advisor coaching you to make your strategic message clearer, more memorable, and easy to repeat. Describe the strategy or decision you need others to understand and share. Ask AI to ground it in a real customer situation, eliminate jargon, and rewrite it as a short, clear story that stands on its own. Listen to see if others can explain it accurately in their own words—that's the sign that your story has become portable.

Move 21: Earn Attention, Don't Steal It

John Arms, a fractional CMO and marketing systems leader, follows a simple mantra: "Lose your self-interest." This idea guides his approach to marketing, communication, and relationships. When you stop focusing on yourself in the exchange, you begin to notice what the other person needs, fears, or is trying to accomplish.

That shift transformed how Arms views marketing. He grew up in a world where, as he described, marketing was built on interruption—the ability to break into someone's day and capture attention. But, he believed there was "a deeper level of connection" that most messages never reached. So he stopped asking, *How do we get noticed?* and began asking, *What is this person already trying to do, and how can we help?* That question changed the message.

It matters even more when pressure increases. When results fall behind, teams often push harder and become louder. Arms recommends taking a pause. "Follow your thoughts to their natural conclusion," he says. If the tactic interrupts, annoys, or creates a transactional relationship, it may grab attention temporarily but will lose trust in the long run.

> **Ask AI for Help:** Prompt AI to think like a customer-focused marketing strategist. Describe your audience, what they're trying to achieve, and the message you want to share. Ask AI to identify where your message feels self-centered or intrusive and to rewrite it so it starts with the audience's problem and minimizes friction. Before sending, ask yourself whether your message helps someone decide faster—or merely adds noise.

Move 22: Pressure-Test for Relevance

Micah Lucas, marketing manager at Cramer and a B2B marketing leader, uses one question to keep communication honest: "So what?"

Lucas considers it a safeguard against noise. "A lot of marketing sounds good," Micah said. "But it doesn't always answer the question, 'So what?' Features get announced. Metrics get shared. But meaning gets lost."

Lucas pushes herself and her teams to dig deeper. "If you can't answer 'so what,' you're not done thinking yet. One pass isn't enough. Neither is two. Each "so what?" brings the message closer to relevance."

For her, clarity isn't about making things simpler. It's about showing respect. "People are busy," she explained. "You have to earn their attention." That means turning updates into results and ideas into decisions—so someone understands what changed, why it's important, and what to do next.

Lucas uses the same discipline when coaching others. "It's not about calling someone out," Micah said. "It's about helping them reach the point faster." When messages answer the question "so what?" they stop sounding busy and begin sounding useful.

> **Ask AI for Help:** Prompt AI to think like a Chief of Staff. I'll paste a draft message and a description of the audience. Run a "So what?" ladder at least 3 times: for each step, restate the message as (1) the decision at stake, (2) why it matters now, (3) the consequence of inaction, and (4) the recommended action. Remove anything that doesn't influence the decision. Then, rewrite the message into two versions: a 10-second opener (1–2 sentences) and a 30-second backup (3–5 sentences).

Move 23: Diagnose the System, Not the Symptom

Phyllis Ferrell, a healthcare executive and transformation leader, believes marketers need to understand the world their customers move through, not just the message they want to deliver. As she put it, "Marketers cannot sit in a cubicle and expect that they're just going to do the arts and crafts piece."

That belief sharpened when she was helping prepare for the launch of a first-in-class Alzheimer's therapy. Her team saw a milestone: enrolling 1,000 U.S. patients in eighteen months. Ferrell saw a warning sign. With millions affected by the disease, she wondered why it took so long. Her marketing instinct told her this was not a normal ramp. It was, in her words, a "canary in the coal mine" for the go-to-market strategy.

When she peeled back the layers of the journey, the real problem came into focus. Only about **10%** of the issue was slow enrollment in the clinical trial. **90%** sat outside it—in delayed diagnosis, weak referral flow, specialty access, and a fragmented care system that patients struggled to move through.

That changed the diagnosis. The barrier was not weak awareness or poor brand messaging. The real competitor was "a completely broken infrastructure" that the product would have to survive in.

> **Ask AI for Help:** Instruct AI to act as a systems-thinking strategic advisor. Describe the outcome you want to influence and what isn't progressing. Have AI map the entire journey, identify all stakeholders involved, and find the real constraint—not just improve your messaging. Then, have it reframe your problem at the system level and suggest a single action to remove the bottleneck. Use the one-sentence diagnosis as your meeting opener.

Move 24: Seek the Friction You're Avoiding

Melissa Chong, a customer success leader at 6sense and founder of Digital Grow, has seen what happens after the sale when promises are tested against real workflows, constraints, and frustrations. That perspective has shaped how she considers customer insight. She also understands why teams avoid the toughest conversations. As she put it, "There is a fear of the customer." She added, "Teams need to ask, do we have a very balanced view?"

Too often, the answer is no.

Teams claim they want to understand customers, but they usually focus on advocates, power users, and those who already agree. They gather feedback from the safest voices and avoid those most likely to challenge their views. Chong sees this pattern often. Teams talk *about* customers all day but hesitate to engage *with* the unhappy, skeptical, or disengaged ones.

That avoidance creates blind spots. Messaging sounds polished but disconnected. Value propositions reflect internal language rather than real customer experience. The story that helped win the deal no longer matches the reality of using the product.

Chong encourages teams to confront the friction they tend to avoid. The goal isn't to provoke conflict unnecessarily but to identify what is broken, unclear, or missing.

> **Ask AI for Help:** Prompt AI to think like a skeptical customer advocate whose role is to uncover overlooked flaws. Describe the specific product, campaign, or initiative you're working on, along with the types of customers or stakeholders whose feedback you usually trust (such as power users, satisfied clients, internal sales teams, or executive sponsors). Ask AI to identify which voices are missing, generate five questions for skeptical or dissatisfied customers, and reveal the assumptions you might be protecting. Then review support tickets, churn notes, reviews, or sales objections to test those assumptions. Use the one-sentence uncertainty statement as a sign of intellectual honesty.

Epilogue: Quiet Progress

A week later, Nala realized the budget shift mattered, but it wasn't the only win.

What stayed with her was what had changed in the room. In the past, leadership meetings felt like theater: dashboards, polite nods, then the same decisions repeated. This time, the room moved because she and Mia had done the invisible work first. They hadn't just brought evidence. They'd given people a clearer way to make sense of it.

Nala noticed the shift in small moments. A sales director stopped repeating "The flagship drives pipeline" and started discussing late-stage enablement as something the team should test more seriously. That wasn't a new dashboard. It was a new line of thinking—simple enough to travel without her in the room.

Nala always believed credibility came from being thorough. More slides. More backup. More proof. She learned that being right isn't the same as being heard. So before her next update, she wrote three lines: what we agree on, what may no longer be true, and what we should do next. OODA to think. SCR to speak.

When the meeting ended, she noticed something new. She left feeling less like she had to prove she belonged there—and more like she knew how to help.

Works Cited

Association of American Colleges & Universities. (2018). Fulfilling the American dream: Liberal education and the future of work - 2018 employer research report. AAC&U.

Coram, R. (2002). Boyd: The fighter pilot who changed the art of war. Little, Brown and Company.

Exasol. (2021, July 13). 93% of IT decision-makers agree embracing data storytelling is the secret to boosting revenue. Business Wire.

Hickman, T., & Stoica, M. (2023). Employer's perception of new hires: What determines their overall satisfaction with recent graduates? The Journal of Research in Business Education, 63(1), 6-23.

Kovacs, I., & Vamosi Zarandne, K. (2022). Digital marketing employability skills in job advertisements - must-have soft skills for entry-level workers: A content analysis. Economics & Sociology, 15(1), 178-192.

Management Consulted. (2025, October 20). McKinsey SCR framework: What it is & how to use it. Management Consulted.

Mercado, J. O., & Mercado, R. E. (2025). Gap analysis of unemployed business graduates' employability skills and industry preferences. Scientific International (Lahore), 37(2), 95-102.

CHAPTER 6: WISDOM BEFORE STRATEGY

"The first principle is that you must not fool yourself—
and you are the easiest person to fool."
—Richard Feynman

Field Story: When The Room Stopped Nodding

Anthony had the dashboard open before anyone asked. He convinced himself it was preparation, not fear.

The weekly growth review brought together marketing, sales, and finance in one room. Anthony was the intern, but his manager asked him to present because he had built the report.

He clicked to the first slide. "Our cost per lead is down 17 percent," he said. "Traffic is up. Conversion rate improved. Engagement is stronger across the landing page flow."

A few heads nodded. Someone said, "Nice."

Then the CFO leaned forward. "Good work," she said. "Now help me understand something. Where does this show up?"

Anthony clicked ahead. "In pipeline. We've created more MQLs. Sales should have more at-bats."

The CFO didn't move. "Which line moves?" she asked. "Revenue? Margin? Or did we just buy activity?"

Anthony's throat tightened. "More leads should mean more closed-won."

"And if we discount to close?" she asked. "What happens below the line?"

Anthony looked back at his chart like it might give him permission to answer. "I don't have margin impact modeled," he said.

The CFO nodded once. Tough and fair. "And cash?" she asked. "When do we spend—and when do we actually get paid?"

Anthony felt the drop. Not embarrassment. More like gravity. A realization that his story didn't reach the ground. "I don't know," he admitted.

The VP of Sales jumped in. "The leads look solid. Let's keep pressing."

"Maybe," the CFO said. "But if margin is tight, volume can hurt us. And if cash comes in late, growth can strain the business before it helps it."

After the meeting, Anthony sat down and wrote one sentence at the top of a blank page: Which line moves—and when?

Then he wrote his original logic: Engagement up → leads up → pipeline up → growth.

He stared at the arrows. That's not reasoning, he realized. That's a hope wearing a spreadsheet.

That night, he reviewed the company's financials. The income statement was first: revenue at the top, followed by costs and discounts that pushed everything down. Then came the cash-flow statement. The numbers hit harder. A company might seem healthy but still run out of oxygen.

The next morning, Anthony grabbed fifteen minutes with a sales ops analyst. "I'm not trying to look smart," he said. "I'm trying to understand what I missed."

She pulled up the pipeline report and invoicing schedule. "Your lead gen did its job," she said. "But our cash conversion cycle is slow right now. We can't afford bets that pay off a year from now."

Anthony nodded. The numbers hadn't been wrong. His story had been incomplete. Once he saw that, he couldn't unsee it.

The Difference Between Data and Judgment

This is the unseen step in most marketing efforts: transforming information into a decision a cross-functional team can rely on. Data can be precise and still be partial. Judgment is what finalizes the process.

Andy Weiss, a B2B SaaS CMO, accurately identified this problem when I first heard his perspective. His words made me stop scrolling because he pinpointed the exact obstacle Anthony had just encountered. That brief moment led to a longer conversation, and eventually to an interview.

Early in our talk, Weiss revisited a moment that changed his way of thinking. Just after finishing his MBA, he started his first director of marketing role with confidence—and a well-crafted 30–60–90 day plan. "I thought, *I've got this,*" he said. "I had my playbook. I had my first ninety days mapped out."

What he couldn't plan for was timing.

He joined in late 2007. Within weeks, the market collapsed. His company's buyers—mid-level procurement leaders—lost decision-making authority overnight. Purchases shifted to CFOs. Budgets froze. The assumptions behind his plan disappeared. "The decision-making process completely changed," Andy said. "My playbook was off the table."

Andy lasted four months.

That experience forced a reset. "Why didn't this work?" he asked himself. The answer wasn't effort or intelligence. It was rigidity. "Playbooks only work when everything falls into place," he said. "When it doesn't, you're improvising—and that's not scalable."

What replaced playbooks are frameworks and mental models. Andy described shifting from "day-trading"—reacting to short-term signals—to adopting a longer-term perspective inspired by Charlie Munger and Warren Buffett. "I don't walk in with Andy's playbook anymore," he explained. "I walk in with a framework for how to think."

That distinction matters more than ever now. "AI hallucinates," Andy said plainly. "Humans do too." His safeguard isn't more data; it's judgment. Frameworks help him simplify, test assumptions, and remove friction before numbers can create false confidence.

Anthony's moment in the meeting echoes Andy's early stumble. The data was correct. The thinking wasn't complete.

That gap between information and judgment is exactly where science speaks.

Why Data Alone Does Not Build Trust

Anthony's meeting wasn't an isolated case. Research indicates the same trend across the workforce. Employers are frustrated because many cannot consider the business impact of their actions—and communicate it clearly.

Cognitive science helps explain why this is difficult. A May 2025 article on Harvard Business School Online describes the "ladder of inference"—a model that shows how people naturally jump from observations to conclusions without noticing the assumptions along the way (Einstein, 2025). As Harvard Business School Professor Amy Edmondson points out in the article, "Our brains are programmed to take shortcuts to speed up decision-making . . . Jumping to conclusions happens quickly, usually without clear awareness." Judgment appears when you slow down, analyze what you're choosing, question what you're assuming, and consider what must be true for your conclusion to be valid.

That's the main problem with Anthony's elevator-drop moment: the numbers were okay, but the reasoning ended too soon.

Employer research clearly highlights this gap. A 2024 survey sponsored by Hult International Business School (1,600 U.S. employees: 800 HR leaders and 800 recent grads) found that critical thinking is a top skill. In fact, 87% of HR leaders said it's essential—but fewer than half said graduates consistently demonstrate it (Workplace Intelligence, 2025).

The same study also found that 97% of employers prioritize business and technology literacy. In other words, analysis only earns trust when it directly relates to how the company operates—such as revenue, margins, and cash flow timing. That's why data without proper context doesn't build confidence; it simply adds noise. Judgment is what transforms "performance metrics" into a decision the room can support.

Employer surveys confirm that financial literacy is now essential job readiness, not just a "nice to have." The New Hire Readiness Report 2025—published by the U.S. Chamber of Commerce and the College Board and based on a survey of 500 hiring managers—found that 96% say financial literacy skills are valuable for entry-level employees, and 61% rate them as very valuable (U.S. Chamber of Commerce & College Board, 2025).

Labor market data reinforce this trend. The U.S. Marketing Jobs Report Q2 2025, published by Taligence LLC and based on analysis of over 83,000 marketing job listings on the client side, shows that roles directly tied to measurable results—such as product marketing, growth marketing, and analytical functions—are growing fastest and commanding higher pay. C-suite positions increased nearly 35 percent year-over-year (Taligence LLC, 2025). This isn't a creativity penalty; it's a clarity reward. Employers are willing to pay marketers who can connect activity to revenue, profit, and long-term value.

Even experienced marketers often struggle to translate marketing language into financial terms. Research from Perion and Advertiser Perceptions—surveying 167 senior marketing decision-makers in late 2025—found that only 21 percent of marketers feel fully aligned with their CFO on budgets and metrics, and just 22 percent believe they have enough data to justify marketing's value to finance (Perion & Advertiser Perceptions, 2025). As one respondent put it: "If the CMO cannot bridge that gap, it makes their remit that much more challenging."

The science is clear. Insight isn't about having the answer. It's about knowing how to reason when the answer isn't obvious.

Why Finance Sees Your Marketing Plan as a Bet

At Anthony's meeting, the CFO wasn't requesting more charts. She wanted proof that marketing understood the business she was charged with protecting—and the decision she was being asked to make.

Sandy Feriz, a Strategic Finance Leader & Value Creator, made it clear during our conversation: finance doesn't interpret "campaign plan" as just a plan. It sees it as a request for capital, and capital is never neutral. Every dollar spent on marketing is a dollar not used for hiring, retaining customers, fixing operations, paying down debt, or protecting cash. That's why the questions always end up in the same place: revenue, margin, and timing.

Feriz also drew a line most marketers don't see until they're bruised in a budget meeting: the job isn't to "justify spend." The job is to reduce risk while increasing confidence. Strong marketing leaders don't walk into finance conversations with optimism and benchmarks. They walk in with the mindset of an investor: what you believe will happen, what could go wrong, what you'll monitor, and what you'll do if the story changes.

That's where credibility is won.

One factor finance cares about more than most marketers realize is incrementality. CFOs aren't impressed by activity that looks good on a dashboard if it would have happened anyway. The real question is always: What changes because we did this? Compared with doing nothing, what lift should we expect—and how will we know we caused it?

When a marketer can explain how an initiative impacts unit economics, working capital, cash flow timing, and downside risk, the conversation changes. You stop sounding like a cost center justifying a budget. You begin to sound like a growth leader who understands how capital moves through the business—and can be trusted with it.

Financial statements aren't the goal. They are the common language that shows how capital moves, where it gets stuck (in inventory, accounts receivable, and long payback cycles), and how marketing decisions either improve or weaken the system.

To address this, you need to understand the three statements well enough to address the real question behind every finance conversation. If we place capital here, what return should we expect, what risk are we taking, and when do we get our money back?

The CFO Test (3 Questions)

Before any initiative earns budget approval, it must answer three questions that finance is already asking.

- **What's the expected return**—and how will we measure it?
- **What's the downside**—and what are the early warning signs?
- **What's the payback timing**—cash, not just revenue?

If you can answer those clearly, you don't have to "sell" finance. You've already met them where they live.

The Three Documents Every Marketer Should Understand

Before diving into the income statement, balance sheet, and cash flow statement, I want to mention someone who changed my perspective on these financial documents.

I met George Benaroya during my graduate studies at NYU. He's a global CFO and faculty member, but what stood out most was his approachability. George has a rare talent: he translates "finance-speak" into plain English without watering it down. His tutorials on reading financial statements helped me stop treating the numbers as a foreign language and start seeing them for what they are: the operating reality of the business.

More importantly, George enhanced my understanding of the connection between CFOs, finance, and marketers. Marketing isn't just about "spend." It's about capital allocation. When we request a budget, we're asking the people responsible for safeguarding cash, margin, and timing to take a risk with us.

That's the purpose of this section. Financial statements are the common language that allows us to earn trust—and demonstrate that we understand what the business is safeguarding.

Three Documents, One Story

Financial statements aren't mysterious documents meant to confuse you. They are stories that reveal a company's health through numbers. Once you grasp the story behind them, you can understand any company's story.

The income statement (also known as a Profit and Loss Statement or P&L) displays performance over a specific period, usually a quarter or a year. Revenue is listed at the top. Costs and expenses are subtracted as you go down. The net income at the bottom shows the result. When a CFO asks, "Where does this show up?" she's asking a combined question: which line changes—revenue, gross margin, or operating expense—and when?

The balance sheet is a snapshot of a specific moment. It shows what the company owns (assets), what it owes (liabilities), and the difference between them (equity). This document reveals financial strength and the ability to invest. It also indicates where capital is tied up—such as accounts receivable, inventory, or deferred revenue—and whether marketing decisions will increase or decrease the business's flexibility.

The cash flow statement tracks actual cash movements. Profit and cash aren't the same thing. A company can show profit while running out of cash. When you understand cash flow, you understand why finance sometimes says "not now" to good ideas. Timing is a risk factor: **when you pay** for growth and **when you collect** from it are rarely the same moment.

A simple map helps:

- **P&L:** What line moves—revenue, margin, OpEx?
- **Balance sheet:** Does this affect working capital (AR, inventory, deferred revenue)?
- **Cash flow:** When do we spend vs. when do we get paid?

The Metrics That Connect Marketing to Money

Five metrics connect marketing efforts to financial results. Learn them, and you'll speak the CFO's language.

Customer acquisition cost (CAC) measures the expense of gaining a new customer. Divide sales and marketing costs by the number of new customers acquired. If you spent $100,000 and gained 500 customers, your CAC is $200. This figure serves as your accountability metric, but it's not fixed forever. CFOs will ask which CAC you are referring to: paid-only or fully loaded, gross adds or net adds, and whether the spend and customer counts are from the same period. The variation influences decision-making.

Customer lifetime value (LTV) explains what CAC alone cannot: how much gross profit that customer generates. If a customer spends $50 per month, stays an average of twenty-four months, and your gross margin is 60 percent, the LTV is $720. The relationship between LTV and CAC determines whether your marketing economics are effective. A common benchmark is: LTV should be at least three times CAC.

Payback period indicates how long it takes to recover your investment in cash, not just in feelings. If your CAC is $200 and each customer brings in $50 in gross profit each month, the payback period is four months. After this, the customer starts to contribute to profit. A shorter payback period means less risk and quicker reinvestment.

Margin is what's left after costs—but which margin? It depends on the question. Gross margin subtracts direct product costs. Contribution margin subtracts variable costs of acquiring and serving customers. Operating margin subtracts overhead. A campaign might increase revenue but reduce margins if it requires deep discounts. Volume isn't always profitable.

Cash timing refers to when money actually moves. A sale recorded today might not result in payment for sixty days. Meanwhile, you've already paid for ads, salespeople, and infrastructure. The cash conversion cycle measures how long it takes to turn cash into inventory and then recover it. When the sales ops analyst told Anthony, "We can't afford experiments that pay off a year from now," she meant this.

And woven throughout everything is the financial question marketers need to answer: Is the impact incremental? Would this revenue have occurred anyway? If not, what's the lift, what's the proof plan, and what are the guardrails if outcomes fall short of expectations?

If you can read the statements and speak to these metrics clearly, you'll stop negotiating for budget and start earning it.

Knowing these metrics matters. But knowing them doesn't automatically protect you from the mistake Anthony made. He had numbers. He had a story. What he didn't have was awareness of how quickly the mind moves from observation to conclusion — and how invisible that leap feels from the inside. That's not a finance problem. It's a human one. And it has a name.

Why Smart People Jump to Conclusions

You've done this. Everyone has. You looked at a set of numbers, formed a conclusion, and by the time you were presenting it, you'd forgotten it was ever a conclusion. It felt like a fact. That gap between what you observed and what you decided it meant is where most analytical mistakes live.

Figure 2 The Ladder of Inference.

Organizational psychologist Chris Argyris called it the Ladder of Inference. Peter Senge brought it to a wider audience in *The Fifth Discipline* in 1990. The model is old. The trap is permanent.

The ladder illustrates how we move from raw data to action, often so quickly we don't notice each step. At the bottom rung is observable data: what's available to everyone in the room. The next rung is selected data: what you decide to focus on. As you climb, you assign meaning, make assumptions, draw conclusions, form beliefs, and finally take action.

The problem isn't the climbing. It's that you forget you climbed at all.

Even worse, your existing beliefs shape which data you reach for next, creating a self-reinforcing loop. You see what you expect to see. You interpret it the way you always have. And you call this "analysis."

We don't just climb quickly. We climb defensively. In any environment where your competence is being evaluated — a meeting, a presentation, a Slack thread where a senior leader is watching — your brain starts protecting your identity before it finishes analyzing the data. You present conclusions as facts. You filter out signals that complicate the story. You tighten the narrative. This isn't dishonesty. It's a normal response to social risk. But it's also how smart, well-prepared people walk confidently into avoidable mistakes.

How Anthony Mistook Signals for Growth

Look at what happened in that conference room.

Anthony observed data: cost per lead decreased, traffic increased, and conversion improved. He selected those metrics because they supported his narrative. He interpreted them as evidence that the campaign was succeeding. He believed leads would convert to revenue. He concluded the business was growing. He presented with confidence.

Anthony wasn't just presenting performance. He was protecting an identity — *I'm the intern who delivers.* That made it harder to stop and ask the one question that mattered: *What if my story is wrong?*

The CFO's question, "Where does this show up in revenue?" pulled him back down the ladder. She wasn't being difficult; she was asking Anthony to show his work on the step he'd skipped: the bridge between "engagement up" and "growth."

That bridge runs through a system Anthony hadn't modeled. Revenue lags. Sales cycles stretch. Pipeline clogs. Discounts erode margin. Cash arrives later than costs.

Anthony's metrics were accurate. His model of how those metrics would behave over time was not. He saw leading indicators and assumed they would flow smoothly into outcomes.

Climbing Down Before You Climb Up

The discipline of descending the ladder involves three questions. Ask them before you present — not after.

What data am I missing — and what data am I ignoring? Anthony's dashboard didn't show the impact on margins, cash timing, or conversion rates by segment. Some data wasn't available. Some data wasn't selected. Both create blind spots, but only one of them is within your control.

What meaning would someone with different responsibilities assign to this data? The CFO saw the same metrics and thought about cash constraints and margin pressure. The VP of Sales saw pipeline capacity and cycle time. The head of customer success saw onboarding load and churn risk. Same data, different meanings.

What assumptions am I making that I haven't tested? Anthony assumed leads would convert at historical rates, that more volume would mean more profit, and that the business wanted growth at any cost. None of these were facts. They were beliefs assembled quickly and presented as conclusions.

Here are two questions that break the ladder before it breaks you:

- What evidence would convince me I'm wrong?
- What would we expect to see if our actions had no effect at all?

These aren't rhetorical exercises. They're the difference between analysis and advocacy. If you can't answer both, you're not ready to present. You're ready to defend a story you already believe, which is a different thing entirely.

When Activity Looks Like Growth

The Ladder of Inference connects to a deeper problem: most marketing "insights" are correlations masquerading as causation. Two things happen at the same time, and the brain reaches for a story that links them, especially when that story confirms what you were hoping for.

Here's a current version of this trap. Your AI-generated content program shows strong engagement metrics — session time up, pages per visit up, social shares increasing. You conclude the content strategy is working and scale the investment.

But what if you climbed back down?

Engagement metrics for AI-generated content often spike initially because the volume increase floods distribution channels. Click-through rates on gated content, qualified pipeline, and revenue attribution tell a different story. The "success" you scaled wasn't generating customers. It was generating activity. And activity, as Anthony learned, is not the same thing as growth.

This is also where the connection to finance becomes concrete. CFOs care about incrementality, not whether activity increased, but whether your actions produced a measurable lift compared to what would have happened anyway. Attribution models provide useful directional evidence. But they don't prove causation on their own. Only careful reasoning, grounded in counterfactuals, honest about disconfirming data, and aware of how systems actually behave over time, reveals what truly caused a change.

The ladder is always there. The discipline is in remembering you're on it.

The Discipline of Breaking Problems to Their Core Truths

Most marketing decisions don't start with original thinking. They start with inheritance. Someone, at some point, decided that monthly promotions drive growth, that trade shows generate pipeline, and that 60 percent of the budget should go to paid media. The decision made sense in its original context. But the context changed, and the decision stayed. What was once a choice became a given.

Figure 3 First Principles in Action

First-principles thinking is the discipline of refusing to accept the given. Aristotle defined first principles as "the first basis from which a thing is known" — the irreducible truths beneath a problem, before assumption and habit have layered over them. Instead of asking *what has worked before*, first principles thinking asks *what must be true* for the outcome we actually want.

That distinction is sharper than it sounds.

Consider a direct-to-consumer skincare brand whose marketing team knows that promotions drive growth. They run monthly 20 percent-off sales, meet revenue targets, and report strong customer acquisition numbers. By every inherited measure, the strategy is working.

First principles thinking begins by questioning the measure. The goal isn't sales — it's profitable growth. So the real question becomes: what must be true for a customer to buy at full price?

Work backward from there. For a customer to pay full price, they must believe the product delivers results worth the cost. They must trust that the price is fair compared to alternatives. And they must feel a sense of urgency driven by desire, not just a discount that expires on Sunday. Now, consider what the brand has actually built: customers who wait. Repeat purchase rates are high — but only during promotions. Contribution margin declines with each campaign. The strategy that seemed like growth is quietly teaching customers not to value the product at its true price.

Once the team clearly understands the mechanics, the solution derives from the problem rather than a playbook. They transition from discount-driven campaigns to building perceived value—using clinical proof points, before-and-after content, and dermatologist endorsements. Promotion frequency decreases from monthly to quarterly. The average order value increases by 25 percent. Margins recover. The discipline wasn't about rejecting promotions; it was about understanding what is sacrificed each time they are accepted—and making deliberate choices.

Many Marketing Decisions Rest on Unquestioned Assumptions

Marketing accumulates inherited assumptions the way a ship accumulates barnacles, gradually, invisibly, until they're slowing everything down. "We need to be on every social platform." "Our industry doesn't respond to content marketing." "We've always allocated 60 percent to paid media." These statements circulate as facts. They're often habits.

First principles thinking involves distinguishing actual constraints from presumed ones. Actual constraints are fixed: your budget, your team's current skills, regulatory limits. Presumed constraints are behavioral: what competitors do, what succeeded last quarter, what the industry deems standard. The first set constrains what is possible. The second set only constrains what you're willing to question.

This is where financial literacy and first principles thinking converge, not as separate disciplines, but as the same discipline applied at different levels. Financial statements reveal the actual economics of a business: what it costs to acquire a customer, what that customer is worth over time, where margin exists and where it leaks. Those numbers are the ground-level truths from which strategy should be built. When you understand them, you're not just optimizing tactics; you're reasoning from the actual structure of the business outward.

How to Rebuild a Strategy from Fundamentals

Think about a B2B software company whose marketing team knows that trade shows are crucial because that's where their industry makes purchasing decisions. The belief has been confirmed by years of attendance, relationships built on the floor, and deals closed months later. It seems like proof. It might just be correlation.

First principles thinking asks a different question: what conditions must exist for a prospect to buy? They need to be aware that a problem exists. They must believe your solution addresses it. They need enough trust in your company to take the risk of recommending you internally. Trade shows can create those conditions. So can other strategies — targeted account-based campaigns, executive roundtables, peer referrals, well-timed content that reaches a buyer the week they're evaluating options.

When you reason from the conditions rather than from the method, trade shows become just one option among many — and not necessarily the most effective one. The same pipeline might be achieved at 40 percent of the cost through channels the team never seriously considered, assuming trade shows.

The discipline isn't about rejecting traditional methods. It's about choosing them — deliberately, with clear reasoning — instead of inheriting them. Any marketer can follow a best practice. Only a marketer who reasons from first principles can see past one.

Anthony Needed All Three Frameworks

Anthony didn't need one framework. He needed all three in sequence.

Financial literacy gave him the language to understand the CFO's question. Revenue, margin, and cash timing. These weren't abstract concepts, but the oxygen keeping the business alive. Without this foundation, he couldn't have known what he was missing.

The ladder of inference explained why his story collapsed. He'd raced from data to conclusion without testing the rungs in between. More importantly, it gave him a diagnostic tool: three questions to ask before anyone else asks them.

First principles thinking gave him a way to rebuild. Instead of patching up his old argument, he could return to fundamentals: What does the business actually need? What must be true for this campaign to matter? What are we assuming that we haven't verified?

The Moves that follow will help you apply each framework. Some focus on financial literacy. Some help you catch yourself mid-climb on the ladder of inference. Others teach you to strip problems down to first principles. Together, they form a toolkit for surviving—and eventually thriving—in rooms where your story will be tested.

Moves to Make Your Thinking More Defensible

Move 25: Learn P&L Statements by Reading Public Numbers

If you want to earn credibility fast, learn to read a profit-and-loss statement, often called a P&L or income statement. You don't need access to your company's internal financials to practice.

You can learn by studying public companies.

George Benaroya, a Global CFO and NYU faculty member, teaches a simple way to read any P&L. He tells students to begin with three sections: **sales, cost of sales, and expenses.** Don't start by trying to understand every accounting term. Start by finding how the company makes money, what it costs to deliver what it sells, and what it spends to run the business.

The basic formula is simple: Sales – Cost of Sales – Expenses = Net Income

Sales may also be called revenue. Cost of sales may be called cost of goods sold or cost of revenue. Net income may also appear as net earnings or net profit after tax.

The names may change, but the business logic stays the same: how much money came in, how much was spent to deliver the product or service, and how much was left after expenses.

Benaroya's next step is where the real learning begins. He teaches students to use percentage of sales as the benchmark. That means you divide each major line by net sales. For example, if a company has net sales of $1,000, cost of sales of $500, and expenses of $400, net income is $100. Cost of sales is 50% of sales. Expenses are 40% of sales. Net income is 10% of sales.

That matters because percentages help you see the shape of the business. A marketer who only sees "$400 in expenses" may miss the point. A marketer who sees "expenses are 40% of sales" starts to understand how leaders compare performance, spot pressure, and make trade-offs.

Here's why this matters for marketers: you're not asking for "budget." You're asking for an investment that must compete with other uses of cash. When you can say, "Here's where the company makes money, where it spends money, and what would have to change for this marketing investment to be worth it," you stop sounding like a cost center. You start sounding like a business partner.

A practical way to start: pick one public company you admire, or one competitor in your industry. Pull its income statement from a public source like the Wall Street Journal, Yahoo Finance, or the company's annual report. Find net sales or revenue first. Then identify cost of sales, operating expenses, and net income. Finally, convert each major line into a percentage of sales and explain the business in plain English, as if you were talking to a smart friend over dinner.

> **Ask AI for Help: Prompt AI to think like the CFO of a public company.** Ask AI to pull the latest income statement from public sources and walk you through it in three parts—sales, cost of sales, and expenses—using simple "percent of sales" math so you can see what really drives profit. Then practice explaining it in your own words and bring one sharp, finance-friendly question into your next meeting.

Move 26: Read a Balance Sheet Like a Cash Flow Detective

Most marketers learn revenue first. Benaroya teaches a different order: follow the cash. A balance sheet shows what the company owns (assets), what it owes (liabilities), and what's left for owners (equity). And it forces one discipline: assets = liabilities + equity. Every decision shows up somewhere.

Why should marketers care? Because budget conversations are really risk conversations. When you understand the balance sheet, you can spot when "spend more" might break the system, and when it's safe to invest for growth.

The mistake is getting lost in dozens of line items. Benaroya tells students to start with five drivers that reveal how the machine runs: receivables, inventory, property/plant/equipment, payables, and debt. Some of these use cash (receivables, inventory, big equipment purchases). Some provide cash (payables, debt). That's the real story: where cash gets tied up—and how the company funds operations while it waits.

His best "quick read" is simple. Look at whether the business collects cash before it pays bills. If payables are healthy relative to receivables and inventory, the company can fund growth without constant cash strain. If not, growth can become a cash trap—even when revenue looks strong.

> **Ask AI for Help:** Ask AI to think like the CFO of a public company. Paste a balance sheet from a public company (or your company, if you have access). Ask AI to walk you through five lines first—receivables, inventory, PP&E, payables, and debt—so you can see where cash is tied up and where it's coming from. Then ask for the top constraints marketing should respect before increasing spend and one action you can take that reduces risk while still driving growth.

Move 27: Validate Before You Declare Ready

Jakki Glivicky Geiger is the chief marketing officer at Arango, where she leads go-to-market strategy for enterprise AI infrastructure.

Earlier in her career, while leading product marketing and field enablement at Informatica, she learned the difference between a strong marketing launch and a revenue-ready launch the hard way.

"We'd done everything right on the product and marketing side," Jakki told me. "The press release went over the wire. Analysts were briefed. The product was ready." From the outside, the launch looked successful. Interest followed quickly. "Customers started calling," she said. "And the sales organization had no idea what to tell them."

That's when the real issue surfaced. Sales hadn't been enabled. There were no demo scripts. Customer success wasn't prepared. "We thought we were ready because the press release went out," Jakki said. "But we weren't ready for customers."

Jakki's team didn't lose the launch because marketing failed. They lost it because the team inferred readiness instead of verifying it.

The assumption felt logical at the time: If product and marketing were ready, the business must be ready. No one stopped to test that belief across sales, customer success, and operations.

That moment reshaped how Jakki approaches launch. "You shouldn't be thinking about product launches," she said. "You should be thinking about revenue-ready launches." For her, readiness means every customer-facing team can deliver on the promise marketing creates—before demand shows up.

"What does success actually look like?" she now asks. Not attention. Not coverage. Outcomes. "If a customer calls, can we sell it? Can we support it? Can we deliver it?"

Her lesson is enduring: Insight isn't just knowing what to launch; it's knowing what the business can actually stand behind.

> **Ask AI for Help:** Prompt AI to act like a logic sparring partner. Describe the action you're about to recommend and the data that's driving your confidence. Ask AI to separate your facts from your interpretations, then list the assumptions you're making between the two—especially what must be true across sales, customer success, and operations for the business to deliver on the promise. Use the output to create a short "revenue-ready" checklist and gather one piece of proof before you claim you're ready.

Move 28: Distinguish Correlation from Causation Before Someone Else Does

"Most marketing 'insights' are correlations that we've dressed up as causation," said a CMO at a medical device manufacturing company and former McKinsey consultant. "We see two things happen at the same time and assume one caused the other."

He was blunt about the risk. "That's the ladder of inference at its most dangerous," he said. "Because once you say *X caused Y*, people start making decisions based on it. Budgets move. Strategy changes. Careers get tied to it."

At McKinsey, he learned to slow that moment down. "We had a rule," he told me. "You never present a causal claim without at least two alternative explanations you've actively tried to rule out." Not acknowledged. Ruled out. "If you couldn't explain why those other explanations *weren't* true, you weren't allowed to say you'd found the cause."

When he moved into marketing leadership, the contrast surprised him. "Teams would say, 'Our competitor launched a product, and our sales dipped that same month—so competitive pressure must be the reason,' " he said. "But timing alone doesn't prove anything."

In one case, several things were happening at once. "We'd raised prices. We'd lost two senior sales reps. We were in the middle of a CRM migration that broke follow-up sequences," he said. "Any one of those could've caused the dip. Or all of them together."

The hardest part wasn't the analysis. "It was admitting we didn't know," he said. "That felt weak in the moment. People wanted answers."

But he learned something else. "Building strategy on guesses feels strong," he said. "Until it fails."

That's the real lesson here. Insight isn't speed. It's restraint. The strongest marketers don't rush to causation—they earn it, before someone else asks the question they can't answer.

> **Ask AI for Help:** Prompt AI to think like a data analyst with expertise in causality. I noticed that [outcome] happened after we [action]. I'm tempted to conclude that our action caused the outcome. Help me think through alternative explanations. What else happened during this time period that could explain the result? What would I need to see to have more confidence that this is causation rather than just correlation? How could I design a test to verify?

Move 29: Strip Problems to Fundamentals Before Accepting Inherited Solutions

Marina Kogan, founder of Brands With Purpose, has learned to be cautious the moment she inherits a marketing plan.

"When I work with a company, there's almost always a plan already running," she said. "Campaigns, messaging, channels—everything looks organized. And because it exists, people assume it's right."

Early in her career, Marina made the mistake of executing inherited plans without questioning them. "I learned the hard way that a plan usually reflects a moment in time," she said. "Different market conditions, different priorities, sometimes even a different customer."

Now, before she commits to execution, Marina validates the foundation. "The first thing I do is ask what problem this plan was originally meant to solve," she explained. "Not the tactic—the problem. Growth? Pipeline quality? Awareness with a specific audience?"

She then pressure-tests the assumptions behind it. "I look for evidence," she said. "Customer interviews, win–loss data, usage patterns. If the plan says we're targeting one Ideal Customer Profile (ICP), I want to see proof that ICP is actually buying."

Her rule is simple. "Execution only works when the thinking underneath it is current," she said. "Otherwise, you're just scaling someone else's guess."

> **Ask AI for Help:** Prompt AI to think like an experienced marketing strategist who uses a Socratic method. For context, I've inherited a marketing plan that includes [briefly describe the plan: target audience, channels, core message, and goal]. Help me validate whether this plan is still relevant today. First, restate the original problem this plan aims to solve. Next, list the key assumptions the plan relies on—about the customer, market conditions, buying behavior, and success metrics. For each assumption, suggest one or two ways I could verify or disprove it using evidence such as customer interviews, data, or internal signals. Then identify which assumptions are most risky if wrong, and explain why. Finally, recommend what I should test or validate before scaling the execution, and which parts of the plan are safest to keep for now.

Epilogue: When the Room Trusted the Thinking

Three weeks later, Anthony presented again. Same room, same faces, different posture.

This time, he didn't open with the dashboard. He opened with the business.

"Before I show the performance metrics," he said, "I want to anchor this in the three questions you're going to ask anyway: what line moves, what could go wrong, and when the cash comes back."

The CFO leaned back slightly.

Anthony clicked to a simple slide. Not fancy. Just the bridge he hadn't built last time. "If this campaign works the way we're assuming," he said, "we should see impact in two places: new revenue and payback timing. Here's what that path requires."

He walked through CAC first, explaining how they calculated it, what was included, and what wasn't. Then LTV using gross margin, not wishful thinking. Then, payback is shown as a range rather than a single heroic number. "I'm not claiming certainty," he said. "I'm showing you what has to be true."

He paused and pointed to two assumptions on the slide.

Assumption one: conversion rates stay the same as we move from early adopters to the next segment. If that drops, the unit economics will fall apart. Assumption two: We can close deals in less than ninety days in Segment B. If sales cycles get longer, cash flow timing becomes a risk.

Then he did something that felt small but changed the room. He clicked to a slide labeled What would we see if this wasn't working?

"If we're wrong," he said, "we'll know early. These are the leading indicators that should move before revenue does. If they don't, we stop. If they do, we scale carefully."

The VP of Sales nodded because it matched the pipeline's actual behavior.

The CFO's expression didn't soften, but her posture did. Tough and fair. The kind of approval you earn. "That," she said, "is a sound business recommendation."

Walking back to his desk, Anthony noticed something else.

The elevator-drop feeling was gone. Not because he had all the answers, but because he'd stopped pretending he did.

He hadn't just shown the numbers. He'd shown the thinking. The tradeoffs. The timing. In this room, that was what trust sounded like.

Works Cited

Einstein, B. (2025, May 6). Understanding how to use the ladder of inference. Harvard Business School Online.

Hult International Business School & Workplace Intelligence. (2025). College graduate skills study: Recent graduates and HR leaders on education and workplace readiness. Hult International Business School.

Perion, & Advertiser Perceptions. (2025). Bridging the CMO-CFO divide. Perion.

Taligence LLC. (2025). U.S. marketing jobs report: Q2 2025. Taligence.

U.S. Chamber of Commerce & College Board. (2025). New hire readiness report 2025: Insights from hiring managers on entry-level workforce preparedness. U.S. Chamber of Commerce and College Board.

CHAPTER 7: TECH FLUENCY & ADAPTABILITY

"Inaction breeds doubt and fear. Action breeds confidence and courage. If you want to conquer fear, do not sit at home and think about it. Go out and get busy."
—Dale Carnegie

Field Story: When a New Tool Makes You Question Yourself

Nala had been in her brand assistant role for two years, long enough to stop asking for daily direction, but not long enough to stop feeling like a fraud.

Her manager, Rachel, had stopped by her desk an hour ago. "We're migrating to a new analytics platform next week. Marketing ops will run training, but I'd love for you to get ahead of it. Pull together a competitive-pricing analysis using the new system before the Thursday meeting. It'll be a good chance to show the team what you can do."

Rachel smiled as if offering a gift. Nala smiled back as if receiving one.

Now she sat alone, the office half-empty in the late-afternoon light, toggling between the platform's login screen and a YouTube tutorial that assumed she already knew what she didn't. The interface looked nothing like the tools she'd used in her graduate program. Every click revealed three more menus she didn't recognize.

She thought about the pricing analysis stored in a folder on her laptop, the one she built last week in Excel, the one Rachel praised. She knew how to do that work but didn't know how to do it here, with this system's buttons, dashboards, and fields that asked for inputs she couldn't name.

Her phone buzzed. A text from her roommate: "Dinner at 7?"

Nala typed back: "Maybe 8. Drowning."

She returned to the screen. The cursor blinked in a search field. She had no idea what to search for.

Everyone else figured this out, she thought. *Why can't I?*

She opened a new browser tab and began searching for a certification course. If she could just get credentialed on this platform, maybe she'd feel less behind. Maybe she'd finally feel like she belonged.

Confidence Usually Comes After You Begin

Confidence builds with taking chances and making mistakes.

By the time I left paramedicine, I was confident amid chaos. Uncertainty didn't paralyze me; it focused me. Assess, intervene, reassess. I'd learned to make decisions with incomplete information because inaction could worsen a patient's condition. That comfort wasn't there on day one. It built slowly, call by call, mistake by mistake, over years of practice in situations where hesitation carried consequences.

What I didn't expect was how little of that confidence would carry over into my first product management role. I knew I could think critically and handle ambiguity. But, I was facing a very different landscape. My intuition and experience were less effective.

The gap between capability and confidence in a new domain is exactly where Nala sits right now. She knows how to build a pricing analysis. She's done it before. What she doesn't trust is her ability to figure out unfamiliar tools, to look competent while learning, and to belong in a room where everyone else seems fluent in systems she's never seen.

If you've ever stared at a new platform, wondering why everyone else seems to get it; if you've ever watched tutorials that assume knowledge you don't have; if you've ever felt like a fraud despite knowing you're capable, you know this feeling. The tool isn't the problem. The gap between what you can do and what you believe you can figure out is the problem.

A CEO mentor told me, "You don't have to struggle alone. You have a whole company of people who need you to succeed. Your work affects them, and they affect you. Ask them for help."

The CEO's advice gave me permission to work cross-functionally: to seek out peers navigating the same uncertainty, asking the same questions, and making the same mistakes, just a few weeks ahead of me. Someone who had just survived the platform migration I was dreading. Talk with someone who bombed a presentation last month and ask them what they wish they'd known.

Find someone just a little further along than you. Not an expert. Not a guru. Just someone who figured out last month what you're struggling with today. Learn from their stumbles, not just their successes. Let their survival be proof that you can survive too.

Nala hasn't learned this yet. She's still at her desk, alone, convinced that everyone else received instructions she somehow missed. She's wrong about that, but she won't know it until she asks.

Why Tool Mastery Is the Wrong Goal

You know the feeling. A new platform lands in your workflow. Another dashboard. Another login. Another interface.

It's not just the tool. It's the pace of change under it. What felt manageable six months ago now feels bigger, messier, and harder to predict. That pressure is real.

The problem is not your lack of effort. It is the scale and churn of the technology itself.

The MarTech Map, also known as the Marketing Technology Landscape, was created to help marketers make sense of a fast-growing software world. In 2025, it included 15,384 solutions, up from 14,106 the year before. The same year, the curators reviewed more than 11,000 submissions, added 2,489 tools, and removed 1,211 that had disappeared. Since 2011, the category has grown from 150 solutions to 15,384 (Brinker & Riemersma, 2025).

That should change how you think about readiness.

No one is mastering 15,384 tools. No one is even mastering a meaningful fraction of them. If your strategy is to keep stacking certifications and hoping you eventually feel caught up, you are running a race with no finish line.

Your advantage will not come from knowing every platform. It will come from becoming the kind of person who can learn new tools quickly, stay calm when things change, and keep sound judgment when the interface, workflow, or rules shift again.

That is why tech fluency matters. Employers expect it. In one national study, 97% of HR leaders said it is important for new hires to have a basic understanding of technology topics such as AI and data analytics. The same study found that 86% of recent graduates believe AI will disrupt their work within the next one to two years, though only 23% feel fully prepared. It also found that 37% of employers would prefer AI or robots over hiring recent graduates for some basic tasks (Workplace Intelligence, 2025).

So yes, the pressure is real. Some of the early work that once helped people build confidence is being automated. Tool knowledge is not the same as adaptability.

Tools change too fast for static knowledge to carry you very far. Dashboards get redesigned. Features move. Workflows break. Integrations fail. AI tools improve, merge, or disappear. In that kind of environment, employers do not just need people who know the current platform. They need people who can stay effective when the current platform becomes outdated.

Research points in that direction. Foundational skills help people remain effective over time because they transfer across roles, systems, and expectations as they evolve (Hosseinioun et al., 2025). Research on employability skills also shows that employers consistently value adaptability and problem-solving, as these skills transfer across jobs and changing environments (Tushar, 2023).

One helpful way to understand adaptability is through the Adaptive Performance Model, developed by industrial-organizational psychologists Elaine Pulakos and her colleagues while studying how people stay effective in rapidly changing environments (Pulakos et al., 2000).

The model is widely used in military, emergency response, and complex organizational settings where people must perform under uncertainty and rapid change. You don't need the full theory to gain its benefits. The core idea is simple: people who remain effective when conditions change rely on a small set of repeatable behaviors. Three of these behaviors are most important for marketers navigating new technologies.

First, they solve problems creatively. When a tool doesn't do what they need, they don't give up out of frustration. Instead, they look for a workaround. They search for the error. They test another approach. They see the constraint as a puzzle, not proof of incapability.

Second, they operate under uncertainty. They do not wait until they understand every feature before engaging with the system. Instead, they start with the small task in front of them. They learn enough to move forward. Then they build from there. In fast-changing environments, progress usually comes from action, not from waiting to feel fully ready.

Third, they keep learning without turning confusion into shame. New tools make almost everyone feel temporarily incompetent. Adaptive people also feel that discomfort, but they interpret it differently. They see it as part of the process, not a verdict on their ability.

That is a better definition of technological adaptability than "knowing the tools." It is what you do when you do not yet know the tool.

Your degree was never going to cover every platform you would encounter. No academic program could keep up with this level of technological change. The gap is real, but it is not mainly a gap in software exposure. It is a gap in learning method, confidence under uncertainty, and repeated practice adapting in real time.

That means adaptability is not a trait you either have or do not have. It is a set of behaviors you can build.

When a new tool appears, start smaller than your anxiety suggests. Ask what problem the tool is meant to solve. Complete one useful task. Write down what confused you, what worked, and what changed from the last system. Ask someone experienced for their top two shortcuts. Compare the new workflow to a tool you already know. Create your own method for learning instead of waiting for confidence to come first.

Leaders should pay attention here, too.

You cannot say adaptability matters and then punish the behaviors that produce it. Learning new systems requires imperfect first attempts, visible questions, small mistakes, and moments where people are slower than usual. If your culture treats those moments as weakness, you are discouraging the very capability you say you want.

If you want adaptable marketers, reward learning velocity along with polished execution. Make room for low-risk experimentation. Let people share what they tried and what they learned. Normalize early confusion before high-stakes performance. Do not just hire for adaptability. Build an environment where it can grow.

The lesson is simple, even if living it is not.

Technological fluency is not about mastering every new platform that appears. It is about learning how to respond when the platform changes, the workflow breaks, or the old playbook stops working. That is a learnable skill. And in a world where the tools keep changing, it may be the most valuable one you build.

When Your Culture Punishes Learning

Not every environment allows visible risk-taking. If yours punishes mistakes, adapt your approach.

Experiment privately before publicly sharing results. Frame the initiative as risk reduction: "I tested whether this could cut reporting time" lands better than "I want to try something new."

Find one ally who values clarity over speed, someone who can vouch for your judgment when you need cover. Document your reasoning before you act so a failed experiment appears as diligence, not recklessness.

The goal isn't sneaking innovation past gatekeepers. It's building adaptive capacity within whatever constraints you face, so that when your latitude expands, your skills are ready.

The Gap Between Knowing and Starting

Knowing what to do and believing you can do it are not the same.

You just read about adaptive behaviors: creative problem-solving, navigating uncertainty, learning new technologies, and managing stress. On the page, they can feel straightforward. You may have read them and thought, "That makes sense. I should do that." But tomorrow is the real test.

When you open an unfamiliar platform, will you begin? Or will you feel that familiar tightness in your chest, search for another tutorial, and wait until you feel ready?

Psychologist Albert Bandura coined the term for the gap between knowing and doing. He called it self-efficac**y, the belief** in one's ability to succeed at a specific task (Bandura, 1977). Self-efficacy is not self-esteem. It is not swagger. It is not a vague sense of confidence. It is your belief that you can handle the challenge in front of you.

That belief influences behavior more than most realize. It explains why two people with similar training might respond so differently to the same new tool. One explores, experiments, and accepts mistakes as part of learning. The other hesitates, avoids, and waits for formal training that might never happen. The difference isn't always knowledge; often, it's belief.

Some readers might recognize part of this feeling as impostor syndrome. That experience is related but different. Impostor syndrome makes you question whether you belong or whether your success is truly deserved. Self-efficacy, on the other hand, is more specific and practical. It affects whether *you* believe you can complete the task at hand. This difference matters because you must build trust in your ability to get started.

Most graduates recognize that AI is transforming the workplace. Many have already tried using tools like ChatGPT. However, far fewer feel confident in their ability to use them effectively. This highlights more than just a knowledge gap; it reveals a confidence gap.

Bandura identified four main sources of self-efficacy, each offering practical value for marketers navigating technological change.

First, mastery experiences. This is the strongest source. Every time you solve a hard problem, you collect evidence that you can figure things out. Not evidence that you know one specific tool forever. Evidence that you can learn, adjust, and make progress. That is why small wins matter. When you find a workaround, troubleshoot an error, or complete a task in an unfamiliar system, you are doing more than finishing the work. You are building proof.

Second, vicarious learning. Confidence grows when you watch someone like you succeed. Not the polished expert who makes everything look easy. A peer. Someone who was confused, stayed with it, and got better. Their progress makes your own progress feel more possible. Their story helps you see that struggle is not a sign you are behind. It is part of how people learn.

Third, verbal persuasion. Encouragement matters, especially when it comes from someone credible. A manager who says, "You learn fast," or a colleague who says, "You've figured out harder things than this," can reinforce a belief that is still forming. The strongest feedback points to your capacity to learn, not just your current level of skill. "You always figure new systems out" is more powerful than "You're good at this platform."

Fourth, physiological reframing. New tools often trigger stress. Your chest tightens. Your patience drops. You want to close the browser and come back later. Those reactions are real, but they do not have to control the meaning you assign to the moment. Many people read that discomfort as proof that they cannot do the task. A better interpretation is simpler and more accurate: this is what learning often feels like at the start.

That is why self-efficacy matters so much during technological change.

Adaptive behaviors describe what successful people do. Self-efficacy explains why they do it. They have gathered enough evidence from past experiences, peer examples, encouragement, and reframing that they trust themselves to start before feeling completely ready.

You do not build it by waiting for confidence to appear. You build it by acting, noticing, learning, and giving yourself credit for the evidence you are creating. One small experiment. One solved problem. One awkward first try. One moment where you stay with the task instead of backing away.

Over time, those moments add up. And when they do, you stop needing perfect certainty before you start. You begin to trust that even if the tool is new, the learning process is not. You have done this before. You can do it again.

Build Confidence Through Action

Move 30: Stagnation Kills More Dreams Than Mistakes Do

Christina O'Leary spent years building brands in environments where certainty is scarce. Today, as the founder and CEO of Pivotal Success and co-founder and creative partner at a healthcare technology startup, she brings an entrepreneurial spirit to every challenge, making decisions daily without complete information.

When O'Leary talks about fear, she doesn't frame it as something to be eliminated. "You're going to be scared," O'Leary said. "That's normal. But you have to harness it. Being stagnant or afraid to make a decision is what holds you back."

She's watched talented people delay launches, over-polish ideas, and wait for reassurance that never arrives. "A lot of it comes from the fear of rejection or the fear of making mistakes," Christina explained. "People want everything to be perfect before they put it out there."

But in her experience, waiting rarely produces clarity. "If you never launch it, you never get it off the ground," she said. "It's never going to get off the ground."

O'Leary doesn't deny that mistakes happen, especially in digital work. She expects them to. "In the digital world, mistakes definitely happen," she said. "But the difference is that we can respond quickly. We can fix things. We can adjust."

That belief shapes how she moves. Instead of treating early work as a final verdict, she treats it as a starting point. "You just have to move," she said. "Launch it. Get started. See how people react. Learn from it."

> **Ask AI for Help:** Prompt AI to think like a performance coach who helps early-career marketers build confidence through action, not perfection. Describe a situation you're facing, what feels uncomfortable about it, and what's at stake. Ask AI to help you name the fear, choose one small imperfect action you can take this week, and define success as learning rather than flawless performance. Then take the step, notice what you learned, and use that evidence to build momentum.

Move 31: Pick a Category and Become the Go-To Expert

Greg Nagy has spent more than two decades scaling complex health technology businesses. Today, he serves as chief operating officer at MDisrupt, leading commercial and operational growth across AI-enabled, FDA-cleared HealthTech platforms.

Despite that experience, Greg is clear about one thing: No one can keep up with everything.

"You're not going to know everything," he said. "That's just reality."

What he's seen separate adaptable marketers from overwhelmed ones is focus. Greg watched a senior leader enter a new industry with a strong résumé but without deep category expertise.

"They didn't feel confident in that domain," he explained. "When people aren't confident, they make the wrong moves."

Without a foundation, every decision felt risky. Instead of learning, the leader fell back on old playbooks that didn't fit. Greg's advice is straightforward. "Pick something big," he said. "And get really, really good at it."

One category. One system. One domain where you become the person others rely on.

From that anchor, adaptability accelerates.

"You don't say, 'I don't know how to do that,' " Greg said. "You say, 'I'll go learn.' "

Depth builds confidence. Confidence makes learning possible. Once you have that anchor, you can learn new tools each week without feeling scattered—because you know where each fits.

> **Ask AI for Help:** Ask AI to think like a career strategist who helps marketers build expertise over time. Describe your current role, what kinds of marketing work you do, and which topics or industries you want to understand more deeply. Ask AI to help you place yourself on a novice-to-expert continuum in a few possible domains, then choose one to focus on for the next year. Use the output to build a learning plan that helps you move to the next level through study, practice, and visible proof of progress.

Move 32: Use AI to Expand Your Thinking—Not Replace It

Jason Padgett spends his days helping organizations and students learn to work with AI without handing over their thinking to it. As a no-code chief AI officer at Phoenix Paramedic Solutions and an AI educator and senior consultant with Phoenix Solutions Group, he's seen what happens when tools are treated as shortcuts rather than as support.

Padgett uses AI early, when ideas are still forming. "AI helps you explore more ideas faster," he explains. "But it doesn't get to decide what's good." That line matters. Padgett is careful about where AI fits, and where it doesn't. When people accept outputs without questioning them, the work suffers. "You still have to ask: What problem are we solving? Who is this for?" he says. "If you stop asking, the tool is driving."

He's equally direct about platform limitations. Jason doesn't treat a tool's UX as a creative boundary. "If the tool can't do what you need, you work around it," he says. "The tool is there to support the work, not force the work into its design."

For Padgett, adaptability isn't about becoming "the AI expert." It's about staying grounded in your thinking, while using AI to push that thinking further.

> **Ask AI for Help:** Think like an expert coach in adaptive performance and AI-augmented thinking. Your role is to help me expand my thinking and evaluate options, not make the decision for me. For context, I am trying to solve the following problem or task in my work: [Briefly describe the situation, the goal, who the work needs to serve, and any constraints or risks.] I want you to help me think through this challenge from multiple angles. First, ask a few clarifying questions about the problem, audience, and constraints. Then help me examine the situation through several lenses—audience, quality, risk, judgment, and tools. Show me possible options and explain the trade-offs of each, including where AI might help and where human judgment should stay in charge. End by asking me which direction I'm leaning toward and why.

Move 33: Evaluate Tools Like a Strategist, Not a Shopper

A Chief Product Officer and MarTech advisor in the FinTech industry offered a discipline most marketing teams skip entirely. "When someone on my team comes to me excited about a new MarTech tool, I slow the conversation down," the advisor said. "Choosing software without judgment leads teams to inherit complexity rather than solve problems."

The first question, the advisor explained, is never about the tool itself. "I usually start with one question: What problem are we trying to solve right now?"

Not the category. Not the feature list. The business problem — pipeline quality, attribution clarity, content velocity, workflow friction. The advisor's rule: if you can't name the problem in one sentence, you're not ready to look at tools.

From there, the advisor narrows the field fast. Use AI to map the category, yes — but don't stop there. Identify the top five to seven tools that consistently appear in analyst reports, peer recommendations, and practitioner forums, then eliminate anything that doesn't fit your size, tech stack, or maturity level. "Fewer options force better thinking," the advisor noted.

What comes next is where most evaluations go wrong. "I want real friction, not demos," the advisor said. That means trialing the top two or three tools with actual data and actual workflows, looking for where it breaks, what feels heavy, what the team would quietly resist using six months in. "Ease of use isn't a 'nice to have.' I'm expecting adoption and impact."

Before any recommendation is made, the advisor requires one more step: do the homework. Read reviews. Scan Reddit threads. "Look for quiet complaints, not polished case studies."

The goal, the advisor concluded, isn't to pick the best tool. "It's to pick the right one for this moment."

> **Ask AI for Help:** Think like a senior marketing strategist who evaluates technology based on business impact, adoption, and long-term usefulness—not hype or feature lists. For context, I am trying to solve the following business problem in my marketing work: [Describe the problem. For example, pipeline quality, attribution clarity, campaign execution speed, reporting visibility, or workflow friction.] I want you to help me evaluate tools in the [insert MarTech category] category. Start by explaining the core jobs this type of tool is meant to perform and the problems it typically does not solve well. Then identify five to seven commonly recommended tools for companies similar to mine. Help me narrow the list to two or three realistic options by comparing ease of adoption, integration with my existing stack, common complaints from practitioners, and situations where each tool would be a poor fit. Finally, suggest what I should test during a trial to uncover real friction before recommending a tool.

Epilogue: Nala Starts Before She's Ready

It was almost seven when Nala closed the YouTube tab.

She hadn't finished the tutorial. She'd stopped halfway through, around the part where the instructor said, "As you already know . . ." for the third time about something she definitely didn't know.

For a moment, she sat with the discomfort. The platform remained open. The cursor still blinked.

She then opened Slack and searched for Priya's name. Priya had transferred from the analytics team six months earlier. She'd been at the Thursday meeting last quarter when Rachel had demoed the old system—and she'd asked a question that made it clear she'd already been using the new one.

Nala typed: "Hey—weird question. When you first started using the new analytics platform, what confused you most? Rachel wants me to build something in it by Thursday, and I'm staring at it like it's in a different language."

She hit send before she could edit it into something that sounded more competent.

Three minutes later, Priya replied: "Oh, God, EVERYTHING. The dashboard labels make no sense. Want to grab coffee tomorrow morning? I can show you the three things I wish someone had told me."

Nala felt her shoulders drop by an inch.

She looked back at the platform. Still unfamiliar. Still intimidating. But the blinking cursor in that search field didn't feel like an accusation anymore.

She typed the first thing that came to mind—pricing template—and pressed Enter.

Twelve results appeared. She clicked the first result.

It wasn't mastery. It wasn't confidence. It was motion.

Works Cited

Bandura, A. (1977). Self-efficacy: Toward a unifying theory of behavioral change. Psychological Review, 84(2), 191-215.

Brinker, S., & Riemersma, F. (2025, May 6). 2025 marketing technology landscape supergraphic. Chiefmartec.

Hosseinioun, M., Neffke, F., Zhang, L., & Youn, H. (2025). Skill dependencies uncover nested human capital. Nature Human Behaviour, 9, 1063-1074.

CHAPTER 8: HOLISTIC GROWTH

"Efforts and courage are not enough without purpose and direction."
—John F. Kennedy

Field Story: When Effort Starts to Add Up

They ended up at the same table by accident.

Anthony arrived first, laptop open, headphones around his neck, scanning notes he wasn't sure he'd ever use again.

Nala dropped into the chair across from him a few minutes later, coffee in hand, exhaling as if the day had already been longer than it should have been. Mia joined last, setting her phone face down, as if she'd made a decision not to be interrupted.

For a moment, no one spoke.

Anthony broke the silence. "I feel like I'm doing everything right," he said. "Classes. Internship. Side projects. Even posting about what I'm learning." He paused. "But it doesn't feel like it's adding up."

Nala nodded. "Same. At work, I'm trying to look confident. In meetings, I'm careful not to say the wrong thing. At home, I replay everything." She shook her head. "None of it feels fake. It just doesn't feel… connected."

Mia listened. She had learned, over time, that listening was often the most useful contribution. "That feeling doesn't go away just because you get better," she said finally. "Early on, you think growth means adding more—more skills, more proof, more effort. But eventually, you realize the pressure isn't from working hard. It's from pulling in different directions."

Anthony frowned. "So what's the fix? Do less?"

"Not exactly," Mia said. "Do truer."

Those words lingered. Nala leaned back. "I had a moment last week," she said. "Someone asked me for help on a project. I almost said no because I was slammed. But it was the kind of work I actually want to be known for." She smiled. "I stayed late. I was tired—but I wasn't drained."

Anthony looked up. "That's different."

"Yeah," Nala said. "It felt aligned."

Mia nodded. "That's coherence. When how you work, who you help, and why you care stop fighting each other."

Anthony laughed quietly. "I thought holistic growth was about balance."

"It's not," Mia said. "It's about direction."

Integration, Not Addition

The skills discussed in this book—curiosity, grit, empathy, observation, judgment, communication, and adaptability—don't become more effective just by increasing their number. They become more impactful when they start to work together. Without integration, skills accumulate but don't connect. You can do more things, but without clarity on which ones matter most.

Holistic growth is not about adding one more skill to your stack. It is about whether the skills you already have are starting to work together.

That is the shift many marketers miss. They gather frameworks, tools, internships, certifications, and side projects. On paper, they seem to be growing. In practice, many feel scattered—busy but unclear, capable but ungrounded. You can accomplish more and still feel like less of it is adding up.

Early in your career, growth often feels like accumulation. Later, the better question becomes: *What is all of this building toward?* Holistic growth begins when your effort stops pulling in five directions and starts reinforcing a direction you truly want.

A useful word for that is coherence.

You won't hear that term often in business courses. It's not a main idea in most marketing books, MBA classes, or career guides. But it should matter to anyone reading this book because it highlights a problem those sources often overlook: not whether you are learning, but whether your choices and contributions work together in a way that can build over time.

The term has roots beyond business. Medical sociologist Aaron Antonovsky introduced the concept of a sense of coherence in his work on health and human resilience, first in "Health, Stress, and Coping" in 1979 and later in "Unraveling the Mystery of Health" in 1987. In that research, the idea of coherence described whether people found life to be understandable, manageable, and meaningful. I am applying that same idea here to work and career growth.

In this chapter, coherence is less about calm and more about fit. It is the point where who you are becoming, how you create value, and the choices you make stop conflicting with each other.

Three dimensions of coherence matter most: Identity, contribution, and decision.

Identity coherence means your work reflects who you are becoming. You are not building a career based on a version of yourself that feels performative, borrowed, or false.

Contribution coherence refers to how your added value connects to what matters to you. The work may still be difficult. It may still be exhausting. But it no longer feels random.

Decision coherence means your approvals and rejections follow a clear logic. Your choices build on each other rather than canceling each other out.

When those three dimensions align, effort feels like an investment. When they don't, effort feels like extraction. You exert energy, but little of it builds momentum.

That is one of the quiet lies of hustle culture. Hustle culture views growth as adding: more hours, more output, more visibility, more proof.

Holistic growth is about integration. The real question isn't, *How much did I do?* but, *Did what I did move me toward someone I truly want to become?*

Many early-career professionals are not lazy. They are misaligned. They work hard in ways that haven't yet connected.

When the Context Doesn't Fit

Sometimes the obstacle to coherence is not your effort. It is fit.

You can be growing and still be in the wrong place. A role might seem logical on paper but still pull you away from who you want to become. A company can reward output while overlooking development. A culture may look healthy from the outside but quietly train you to perform instead of contribute. When that happens, the issue isn't always a lack of motivation; sometimes, the problem is the context.

Katie Sandoe, D.Ed., a leadership and well-being expert, often notices this tension among ambitious professionals. Many are capable, driven, and outwardly successful, yet feel tired, stuck, or disconnected from their work. She said many younger professionals focus on "the immediacy of the now" and that "what they've not yet fully connected is how a deep sense of fulfillment is a rich and important part of the professional and human experience."

That insight is important because misfit often remains quiet before becoming obvious. It can manifest as Sunday dread that never fully goes away. It can sound like a voice in your head asking why success feels emptier than expected. It can feel like becoming more polished at work but feeling less like yourself. Those signals are easy to dismiss, especially when the job still provides status, income, or momentum. But, they deserve attention.

Sandoe points out that many people only start asking tougher questions after years of trying. They switch jobs, pursue new opportunities, and do what they think ambitious people should do. Then, they realize something still feels off. As she mentioned, people often discover "how important it is that work contributes to something bigger than yourself." When work no longer aligns with your values, growth, or sense of contribution, even progress can start to feel meaningless.

There's no strict rule for when to stay or leave, but better questions exist. Have you clearly identified the problem? Have you tried to improve the situation through honest conversation, changing responsibilities, or shifting support? Are you still learning in meaningful ways? Is the situation progressing at all, or are you just holding on to hope?

If you've genuinely tried, communicated clearly, and allowed the situation time without seeing much progress, the evidence might be telling you something. Coherence sometimes means staying and reshaping your work. Sometimes, it means leaving intentionally, not because you're restless but because the picture has become clear.

Sandoe's advice in these moments is practical. She recommends developing a personal mission, identifying your core values, and creating a decision-making framework. In her view, a personal mission asks what kind of impact you want to have in your professional life. Core values clarify how you plan to make that impact. Then, the focus shifts to what you want to pursue over the next one to three years to achieve that in your career.

That advice reflects a much more intense perspective from Bob Moesta, who said, "I've chosen to pick that as my death date. And so literally I'm here because I only have three thousand days left and I need to impact people." Different words, same goal. Both Sandoe and Moesta emphasize a bigger view for decision-making. Clarity improves when choices are seen as expressions of a broader direction instead of isolated reactions.

It's also important to recognize that coherence isn't always within everyone's reach at all times. Financial pressures, caregiving responsibilities, health concerns, and economic instability can restrict the opportunities for career advancement. What might appear to be a compromise from an outsider's perspective could actually be a smart choice given what this season of life requires. The goal isn't perfection but making progress in the right direction.

Closing the Loop on the T-Shaped Marketer

Becoming a T-shaped marketer isn't aspirational; it's the minimum. When you first picked up this book, that may have felt like a high or abstract goal. Now, you should understand why it's true and what it really takes.

The horizontal dimension of the T—wide awareness across strategy, finance, technology, customer experience, and organizational behavior—stops you from being stuck in just one perspective. It helps you ask smarter questions, work across different areas, and understand your environment without needing to be an expert in everything.

The vertical dimension—deepening expertise in a single area over time—is what builds your credibility. General awareness is useful, but it can't replace the discipline of mastering a craft. Broad knowledge without depth makes you conversational but not trustworthy. Deep knowledge without breadth makes you capable but isolated.

What the T-model doesn't show is what holds the two dimensions together—that's coherence. The T describes the shape of your knowledge, while coherence explains whether that knowledge functions as a system. A T-shaped marketer without coherence has the right skills but in the wrong arrangement. Conversely, a T-shaped marketer with coherence has skills that reinforce each other, a clear direction those skills serve, and the judgment to know when to go deep and when to reach across.

What Experienced Leaders Have Learned

Across many conversations with experienced leaders, a consistent pattern emerged. The people who sustained meaningful careers did not grow faster by doing more. They grew steadier by connecting their effort, values, and contribution. A few themes came up again and again.

On sustainability: Debbie Gainsford clearly states that you do not live to work; you work to live. For her, career sustainability isn't about dialing back ambition; it's about integrating ambition into a life that can actually support it. Passions outside of work, time away, and a genuine support system—these are not just perks but essential. Growth that consumes life ultimately depletes itself. Josh King describes the same idea through rhythm rather than balance. Work and life are never perfectly even, he says, but they can harmonize. The key is recognizing patterns—when intensity is beneficial, when recovery is needed, and how curiosity drives both. He aims to end each week with one new question he cannot yet answer—not as a source of panic, but as motivation for what's next.

On the cost of moving too fast without integrating: Nitin Kartik has observed talented people burn out because they never slowed down enough to process what they learned. They focused on the next success, then the next, until those successes no longer felt meaningful. One leader I spoke with described a former colleague who advanced faster than almost anyone in his group: VP by thirty-two, with every target met and every promotion earned. The speed masked a growing disconnect. The work that once energized him became purely transactional. He could no longer explain why he was doing any of it beyond momentum. When his role was eliminated in a reorganization, he had credentials but no sense of direction. The rebuild took years because he had never developed the internal compass to assess them. Speed without integration isn't efficiency. It's accumulation without purpose. Once lost, purpose is harder to regain than skills.

On contribution: Bob Moesta gauges his life not by titles or awards, but by how many people he can help. He describes himself as a vessel—absorbing ideas, synthesizing them, and passing them along. In his view, knowledge only matters if it benefits someone else. That mindset connects directly to something Micah Lucas said: if she is going to spend forty hours a week with someone, she would rather work with a person who is kind, curious, and easy to collaborate with, even if they are still learning the job. Competence matters, but character counts.

On reflection: Brooke Sellas documents everything—notes, ideas, lessons, missteps. Every few years, she revisits old notebooks, not to critique herself, but to see how far she has come. The effect isn't nostalgia; it's confidence. Reflection turns experience into evidence. Over time, patterns become visible. You start to notice what repeats, what you've outgrown, and what still confuses you. That habit is most important when things go wrong. Coherence doesn't prevent failure; it helps you recover from it.

Mentorship, Reflection, and Recovery

Most early-career marketers lack mentors. They have managers, but that's not the same thing. A manager assesses your work, while a mentor invests in your growth without expecting anything back.

Good mentors rarely make a formal announcement. They are colleagues who ask about what you're trying to learn, not just what you're working on. They are former bosses who check in after they've moved on. They are people a few years ahead who remember what confused them and provide context without condescension.

Finding them requires both visibility and vulnerability. Visibility involves doing work that people notice—not for credit, but because quality draws attention. Vulnerability means admitting what you don't know and asking for help openly. If asking for a thirty-minute conversation feels intimidating, start smaller. Comment thoughtfully on someone's work during a meeting. Send a brief note after a presentation. Ask one specific question in a group setting. These smaller interactions build familiarity before you request something more substantial. When you're ready, being specific helps: "I'm trying to get better at X. Would you be willing to spend twenty minutes talking through how you approach it?" This approach opens more doors than most people expect.

Reflection is just as important. Integration depends on it. Without reflection, progress remains unseen—and unaddressed failure lingers. It builds up as anxiety, defensiveness, and a quiet fear that influences future choices without your awareness.

Sitting with the discomfort of a setback long enough to learn from it is harder than skipping past it. This is how failure becomes growth instead of damage. What actually happened? What was within your control and what was not? What would you do differently, and what would you do the same? These questions hurt more than avoiding them. They are also the reason some people grow while others simply accumulate scar tissue.

Purpose, Discernment, and Saying No

Purpose emerged as a recurring theme in nearly every conversation I had while writing this book. Without a guiding star—values you refuse to compromise—direction slowly fades away. Purpose doesn't usually announce itself; it reveals itself in choices: what you accept and what you turn down, even when the opportunity seems appealing on paper. Work feels meaningful when your actions reflect what truly matters to you.

For early-career marketers, purpose is often discovered rather than declared. You don't need to know your life's mission in your twenties. What you should do is pay attention. Notice which work energizes you and which drains you. Recognize which accomplishments feel hollow and which feel genuine. Observe the problems that hold your interest even when no one is watching. Purpose naturally emerges from these patterns. Over time, the meaning becomes clearer.

This is where the discipline of saying "no" becomes crucial. Early in a career, saying yes is usually beneficial. Yes to exposure. Yes to learning. Yes to opportunities you don't fully understand yet. Those create momentum, and momentum leads to experience.

There comes a point, often sooner than expected, when growth no longer responds to just adding more. Every new commitment starts competing with something else that matters. At that moment, discernment becomes more important than simply being available.

Many early-career marketers stay busy not because the work is crucial, but because the fear of saying no feels overwhelming. Saying yes keeps you visible. It keeps you helpful. It keeps doors open. However, over time, saying yes all the time dulls everything. All tasks begin to seem equally urgent, equally important, and equally exhausting.

Holistic growth introduces a different discipline—the discipline of subtraction. This isn't about disengaging or pulling back; it's about recognizing that focus is a responsibility. If you want to master your craft and be known for something rather than everything, you must decide what no longer deserves your energy. This kind of no isn't defensive. It's directional. It protects learning depth. It protects identity. It makes room for what's next by clearing out what no longer fits.

That said, subtraction carries its own risks. Some people learn the discipline of saying no and overuse it, declining opportunities before they've developed the judgment to evaluate them. Discernment develops through experience, not before it. In the environments most early-career professionals actually encounter—where a manager assigns a project or a professor sets the syllabus—the power dynamics are real. In those situations, the discipline of saying no becomes more nuanced. It might mean negotiating scope rather than refusing outright. It might mean asking what should be deprioritized. These are not refusals; they are negotiations. They create space for conscious tradeoffs rather than unseen ones.

Why Coherence Compounds

Coherence is a competitive edge in a market that's reorganizing faster than most career advice can follow.

The introduction to this book described a labor market doing two things at once: shrinking in areas that rely on routine tasks and expanding in areas that require judgment, adaptability, and connecting marketing work to revenue, margins, and business outcomes. The question raised was whether you would end up on the expanding side or the shrinking side.

Coherence plays a key role in shaping the response. Marketers who understand their core values, goals, and how their work connects to something larger are not only more fulfilled but also more understandable to employers, more trusted by colleagues, and better equipped to contribute in ways that can't be automated. That's where the market is expanding. That's where coherence naturally multiplies.

It compounds personally as well. Marketers with coherence make better decisions because their choices follow a consistent logic. They waste less time on opportunities that don't fit and engage more fully with the ones that do. They build stronger relationships because they are not constantly repositioning themselves—colleagues, clients, and managers know what to expect. This consistency builds their reputation, and a good reputation opens doors that credentials alone cannot.

They recover faster from setbacks because they have an internal compass. When things go wrong, they adjust course and keep moving rather than spiraling into an identity crisis.

A common fear is that coherence leads to slower progress, and that being selective about opportunities will make you fall behind peers who seem to accept everything. This concern is understandable but mostly incorrect. Early-career speed often results in gaining breadth without developing depth. You may have done many things but mastered few. You might have built a network but not a reputation. When it's time to take on larger responsibilities, those who have advanced more deliberately often have clearer stories to tell, stronger skills to offer, and better relationships to rely on.

Careers rarely change because someone learns just one new skill. They change when the skills they already possess start working together.

Move 34: Stay Open Long Enough to See the Better Path

Early in your career, coherence does not always arrive as certainty. Sometimes it shows up as openness. Court Stroud, an NYU clinical assistant professor of integrated marketing and a former media leader with more than two decades of experience across television, radio, print, and digital media, told me he once had a very different plan for his life. He studied broadcast journalism and Spanish literature and fully expected to work in television news. But when graduation came, he was offered a rookie sales job at a Spanish-language AM radio station in Houston—an option he said was "nothing I could have considered." He took it anyway. Looking back, he believes that single act of openness changed his trajectory and helped make him distinctive enough to later attend Harvard Business School. Sometimes coherence is discovered only after you step into something that was not part of the original script. Stroud's deeper lesson is not to drift aimlessly. It is to stay open when life presents a path that might teach you something your original plan could not. As he put it, "When you're open, you hear the bad ideas and the good ideas. When you're closed, you don't hear the bad ideas or the good ideas."

> **Ask AI for Help:** Use this prompt when an unexpected opportunity makes you question whether to follow your original plan or pursue your emerging fit. Prompt AI to think like a career coach, vocational advisor, and trusted mentor for an early-career marketer. For context, I expected my career path to look like [original plan], but now I have an unexpected opportunity in [role, industry, or project]. Help me evaluate whether this opportunity represents a worthwhile growth challenge or a distracting detour. Ask me 7 thoughtful questions about fit, learning, values, long-term potential, and what this path might teach me that my original plan would not. Then assist me in comparing both options and identifying which choice is more likely to support my growth, sharpen my skills, and broaden my perspective.

Move 35: Get Clear About What Matters

Coherence becomes easier when you can identify what matters to you before pressure, ambition, or opportunity start influencing your decisions. If you can't clearly articulate your values, it's much easier to drift into roles, teams, or companies that seem impressive on paper but don't align with who you are or how you want to work. Deirdre Breakenridge has spent over thirty years helping professionals boost their influence through communication. As a storyteller, speaker coach, and communications trainer, she has worked with leaders on aligning their message, presence, and behavior to build trust and lead more effectively. That idea of alignment is important here, too. Holistic growth involves more than just skills; it depends on whether your work truly reflects what you care about.

Breakenridge said many younger professionals are "not really thinking about what it is that they value, and they end up in places that don't make sense for them." Her advice was simple: do a "little ethics test." If someone asked what you value, you should be able to answer in about 30 seconds: "This is what I care about."

That kind of clarity helps you move beyond vague phrases like "good culture" or "meaningful work." It gives you a way to judge fit. If you can name what matters, you are less likely to let other people's priorities quietly choose your path for you.

> **Ask AI for Help:** Prompt AI to think like a career coach, ethics professor, and trusted mentor for an early-career marketer. Help me build a 30-second ethics test for my career. Ask me 8 questions to uncover the values I care about most in my work, the kind of environment that fits me best, and the behaviors or tradeoffs I do not want to normalize. Then help me write a 4–6 sentence statement that begins with 'This is what I care about...' and turn it into a simple decision screen I can use when evaluating jobs, managers, teams, or projects.

Move 36: Strengthen the Human Skills AI Can't Carry for You

Bahriye Goren, a marketing educator and researcher whose work explores compassionate leadership, purpose, and inclusive design thinking, offered a timely reminder for early-career marketers facing the rise of AI. The future will not belong only to those who move fastest with the tools. It will also belong to those who know how to bring judgment, ethics, empathy, and direction to their work.

That matters because it is easy to misunderstand what relevance looks like in an AI-driven market. You might assume your goal is to produce more, automate more, and become more technically skilled than everyone else. Those things are important. But, they don't tell the whole story. If AI can speed up output, then your advantage shifts to work that involves deeper human skills: interpreting what the tool generates, asking better questions, applying judgment, and guiding people toward decisions aligned with strategy and values.

Goren expressed it this way: "Marketers have an opportunity to create value through having a vision, a culture, and a longer-term strategy. With the rise of GenAI, marketers' added value becomes even more important in areas that are harder to automate, including ethics, culture, and vision."

Learn the tools. But, don't neglect the parts of yourself that tools cannot handle. As AI advances, your advantage shifts from doing more to judging better.

> **Ask AI for Help:** Prompt AI to think like a marketing professor, career coach, and chief marketing officer who develops early-career talent. AI is changing the kind of work marketers do. Help me identify the human skills I need to strengthen so I become more valuable, not less. Ask me 7 questions about my current strengths, the kind of marketer I want to become, how I handle ambiguity, relationships, ethics, judgment, and long-term thinking. Then recommend the 3 human skills I should prioritize over the next 90 days, explain why they matter, and suggest practical ways to build them through my current job, classes, projects, or internships.

Move 37: Don't Confuse Promotion with Fit

Brent Roberts, a business leader with experience in military leadership, strategic marketing, sales, and general management, offered a useful warning for ambitious professionals: the next title is not always the next right step. When his team considers promotions, they look for more than talent. They look for proven performance, alignment with the company's values, and evidence that the person actually has the skills to succeed in the new role. As Roberts put it, some people are strong individual contributors but can be "very challenged as a manager."

That matters because early-career professionals often treat promotion as proof. Proof that they are growing. Proof that they are winning. Proof that they belong. But, a promotion can create new problems if it pulls you away from your strengths or places you in a role that does not match how you think, prioritize, or lead. Roberts was blunt about cultural fit, too: "Even if somebody's a superstar talent, but they don't embody those values, they just won't succeed here." Not every impressive opportunity is a good fit.

That does not mean you should avoid challenge. Roberts also said new managers need grace, support, and room to make mistakes because "that's part of the growth process." The deeper lesson is simple: not every promotion is progress, and not every fit comes with a bigger title.

> **Ask AI for Help:** Prompt AI to think like an executive coach, experienced people manager, and trusted mentor who wants to help me grow without drifting into the wrong role. I'm considering a move from [current role] to [next role]. Help me evaluate whether this opportunity is genuine growth or just a more impressive title. Ask me 8 thoughtful questions about my strengths, values, tolerance for ambiguity, ability to prioritize, interest in leading people, response to pressure, and the kind of work that energizes or drains me. Then help me compare the real demands of the new role with how I am wired, identify where the fit looks strong or weak, and suggest what support, training, or boundaries I would need to succeed without burning out.

Move 38: Stack the Odds in Your Favor Before Day One

Vladimir Blagojevic, co-founder of FullFunnel, assists marketing and sales teams in connecting, engaging, and winning the right accounts. His advice for early-career marketers is practical and notably proactive: "Just start learning before you even get there."

That idea is important because many people start a new role expecting clarity to come later. Vladimir's point is the opposite. If you want a better experience and a higher chance to contribute, begin learning before day one. Read reviews. Reach out to users. Ask industry experts for fifteen minutes of insight. Once you're inside, listen to sales calls, onboarding calls, and customer conversations. Build relationships with people in sales, product marketing, and content. Get close to the real work before trying to improve it.

His advice reflects a broader truth about growth. When teams struggle, he says, "Usually, it isn't the tactics, it's usually it's much more fundamental." The same is often true for careers. What holds people back isn't always a lack of hustle or tools, it's a lack of context.

The quicker you understand customers, colleagues, and how work actually flows, the faster your skills become useful. Credibility increases when curiosity appears early.

Ask AI for Help: Prompt AI to think like a marketing leader, onboarding manager, and cross-functional teammate who wants me to ramp up quickly. I'm about to start a role in [company, industry, or function]. Help me improve my chances before day one. Ask me 7 questions about what I already know, what access I have to customer reviews, sales calls, onboarding materials, company content, public information, and internal stakeholders, and what I most need to learn. Then create a 14-day learning plan to help me understand the product, the customer, the buying journey, key cross-functional relationships, and the questions I should ask so I can become useful faster.

Move 39: Answer "Tell Me About Yourself" with Direction

Scott Hurst, a healthcare CEO, offers a better answer to "Tell me about yourself" than most career guides do. He recommends mentees start with an elevator pitch. Not a polished slogan. Not a list of past jobs. A clear statement of what they plan to do. As one of his early mentors told him, "If you can't tell somebody in 15 seconds what you intend to do, then you need to figure that out first."

That matters because many early-career professionals answer this question by describing where they've been instead of where they're headed. They recite a résumé, listing majors, internships, and software tools. None of that is useless, but it rarely makes you memorable. Scott's point is that clarity leads to better help, better conversations, and better opportunities. If people understand the role you want to play, they can connect you, challenge you, and guide you more effectively. Scott's own version was simple and specific: he wanted to be "the guy that helped doctors and suits finally talk the same language." That throughline shaped his decisions even as his titles changed.

The best response to "Tell me about yourself" does three things: it identifies the problem you care about, the people you're aiming to help, and the role you want to play.

Ask AI for Help: Prompt AI to think like a hiring manager, career coach, and executive mentor. Help me craft a clear, natural answer to the question 'Tell me about yourself.' Have me answer 7 questions about the problems I want to solve, the people or customers I want to help, the strengths I want to be known for, and the direction I want my career to take. Then, write three versions of my answer: one for an interview, one for a networking conversation, and one for a mentor. Keep each version specific, warm, and under 90 seconds.

Move 40: Build Your T-Shape on Purpose

I feel honored to present the final Move in this book.

My advice is to stay open to moving within the organization whenever the opportunity makes sense. McKinsey has noted that job rotations can help people develop both the breadth and depth of skills needed over time. That insight aligns with my own career more than any neat plan ever could.

I did not grow by staying in one lane. I grew by moving through product management, marketing, sales, customer experience, and strategic relationships, and even by taking a one-year sojourn that broadened how I viewed work and people. Each stop contributed something different. Some experiences deepened my craft. Others expanded my perspective. Together, they made me more valuable.

That's why intentionally developing your T-shape is essential. Depth is important. You need a craft worth recognition, and broad skills are also vital. You become more valuable when you understand how your work connects to customers, revenue, operations, and those around you.

So, don't see movement as a distraction if it sharpens your judgment and broadens your understanding of the business. Sometimes, the best way to become more yourself at work is to step into roles that show you how the whole system fits together.

Ask AI for Help: Prompt AI to think like a chief executive officer, career coach, and cross-functional business leader who develops T-shaped talent. Help me intentionally build my T-shape. Ask me 8 questions about the craft I want to deepen, the strengths I want to be known for, the parts of the business I understand least, the functions I'm curious about, and the roles or projects that could broaden my perspective. Then help me find 3 smart ways to expand across the organization without losing depth and explain how each move could strengthen my business acumen, judgment, and long-term career path.

Epilogue: The Marketer You're Becoming

The next week, the shift was small but visible.

Anthony stopped saying yes to every opportunity that seemed impressive from afar. Instead, he began choosing work that refined his skills. He spent more time studying how to craft strong messages, ask better questions, and understand customers. His ambition remained, but it became more focused. He was no longer trying to gather proof that he was serious; he aimed to become genuinely useful in lasting ways.

Nala became more selective too. She still cared about doing excellent work, but she paid closer attention to the kind of marketer she was becoming through that work. She leaned more into the parts of the craft that required judgment, empathy, and clear thinking across functions. She realized that being T-shaped wasn't just about building depth in one area; it was about making that depth more valuable by connecting it to sales, customers, leadership, and the broader business.

Mia, meanwhile, became more disciplined about her direction. She continued honing her ability to recognize patterns, frame problems, and bring clarity into the room, but she also grew more intentional about where she invested her time. She was no longer treating every open door as a sign to walk through it. She was learning that maturity meant protecting the conditions that allowed her strengths to deepen and connect.

None of them had arrived, but their growth was starting to take shape. They were becoming less reactive, less scattered, and more intentional about the crafts they aimed to master and the broader business context they wanted to grasp. That is part of what it means to become T-shaped. Not just to learn more, but to learn in a way that helps your skills stay connected.

Works Cited

Antonovsky, A. (1979). Health, stress, and coping. Jossey-Bass.

Antonovsky, A. (1987). Unraveling the mystery of health: How people manage stress and stay well. Jossey-Bass.

CONCLUSION

What You Were Really Building

By the time you reach this page, you've read a book about marketing, and if the book did its job, you already realize that's not completely accurate.

You read about campaigns, frameworks, and the realities of the job market. You followed Anthony into a meeting where the language felt unfamiliar. You sat with Nala while she replayed every word she said in a room where she wasn't sure she belonged. You watched Mia resist the urge to give answers and instead asked better questions.

Those weren't marketing stories. They were stories about what it takes to earn people's trust. That was the true focus all along.

What the Market Now Demands

You entered this field during a structural shift, not a temporary disruption.

The funds that used to flow back to shareholders are now being redirected—quickly and at scale—into artificial intelligence infrastructure. The effects aren't abstract. They're already visible in how teams are formed, which roles are funded, and what hiring managers mean when they say they want someone who "can think."

The market isn't asking for better tool operators. It's asking for people who can work with incomplete information, navigate cross-functional tension, connect marketing activity to business outcomes, and make decisions that hold up under scrutiny. Not someday. Now.

That's a high bar for someone early in their career. But it's also a reachable one—if you understand what's actually being asked of you.

Employers aren't searching for a finished product. They want evidence of growth. They look for how you learn when the situation feels uncomfortable. They want to see how you manage a problem that doesn't have an answer in the back of the chapter. They want to know whether you can be trusted with messy, unstructured, genuinely tough work—not just the visible tasks.

That's the opportunity before you. The marketers who will be most valued in the next decade aren't the ones who know the most platforms. They're the ones who can think clearly, communicate honestly, connect across functions, and continue growing as the ground keeps shifting.

What It Means to Become T-Shaped

T-shaped isn't a credential. It's not a certification you can add to your LinkedIn profile. It's a way of operating.

The vertical stroke of the T is your craft. It's what you're willing to go deeper on than most people in the room. The place where your contribution isn't just enthusiasm—it's expertise. That depth is what gives you something real to offer. It's what earns you the right to be heard.

The horizontal stroke is your reach. It's what happens when you stop treating your job as a lane and start treating it as a position within a larger system: When you learn how sales thinks before you criticize the pipeline, when you study a financial statement not because you're asked to, but because the decisions you're trying to influence are made in financial language, and when you walk across the hallway—or the org chart—to understand a function before the situation forces you to.

Depth gives you substance. Breadth gives your substance reach.

But the part that doesn't get enough attention—the part this book has been quietly leading up to from the first chapter—is the third dimension.

Integration.

Depth without breadth is a silo. Breadth without depth is noise. But, when curiosity connects to empathy, and empathy guides your communication, and judgment is the foundation, sharpened by grit—something different begins to happen. You stop feeling like just a collection of skills. You start feeling like someone others can truly rely on.

That's the difference between someone who knows marketing and someone who can carry it. That's what T-shaped really means.

Why This Journey Is Iterative, Not Linear

You won't progress through this framework in a straight line. You won't finish Thirst to Learn, check it off, and then move on to Grit. You won't reach Holistic Growth after completing the other six. That's not how this works.

You'll build Grit in a situation meant to test your communication skills. You'll learn something about Wisdom in a conversation you thought was only about empathy. You'll see that the Tech Fluency you gained in one role helps you understand how you relate to people in the next. Growth doesn't announce itself. It quietly appears later, when you look back and see that you've handled things differently than you would have six months ago.

That's the nature of real development. It isn't flashy. It rarely feels like progress while it's happening. It looks like sticking with a tough problem when the easier option would be to pass it on. It looks like asking a question in a meeting instead of just nodding along. It looks like choosing the project that teaches you something over the one that seems impressive.

Quiet moves. Real compounding.

There will be times when one aspect demands most of your focus. Times when you're developing depth in your craft at the cost of everything else—and that's okay. Times when you're expanding into breadth, feeling uncomfortable and uncertain, wondering if you've stretched too far. Times when the work is about integration: bringing together what you've gathered and figuring out how it all fits.

None of those seasons are wrong. All of them are the job.

Let me leave you with something more personal.

I was fifty years old when a board decision ended eighteen years of my professional life in a single meeting.

The last three years, I led the marketing efforts for a healthcare startup spun out of a multinational company. We aimed to revolutionize how the healthcare industry trains its staff. The goals were bold—achieve 100% growth year after year. I assembled the team. We developed the products. We sought out customers. Then the board reviewed our division, considered their priorities, and made a decision that had nothing to do with our hard work or whether we were on the right path. They eliminated us.

It was the only time in my career I was let go, and at the eighteen-year mark, it came as a complete surprise. The nine months that followed were their own kind of curriculum.

I had been delaying graduate school for years—actually, decades. Other commitments always seemed to get in the way. I was on the road more than 150 nights a year, building things, moving quickly, with a constant reason to postpone the degree. The sudden quietness of unemployment took away every excuse. So, I enrolled. And I soon realized that I was the oldest person in the room by a large margin.

Most of the time, the generational gap was enlightening. Sometimes, it reminded me why experience holds a value that can't be downloaded.

Once, during a team project, I started checking the math. A classmate stopped me. "This is not a finance class, David," she said. I laughed. To myself, mostly.

Because every business decision is a finance class. Every campaign, every headcount request, every product launch, every pivot. The failure to recognize that—and to treat marketing as something that operates within the realm of money—is exactly the gap this book aims to fill.

I didn't return to school just because the calendar finally cleared. I went back because I wanted to teach. I wanted to share everything I had learned—the eighteen years, the startup, the journey, the board decision, the nine months of figuring out what's next—and pass it on to people starting careers I recognized. This book is that project, made larger.

The students I teach now are Anthony, Nala, and Mia, sitting in front of me with real names and real doubts, all hiding the same quiet question beneath it: "Am I ready for this?"

My answer always remains the same. You are not falling behind; you are aligned. The discomfort you experience isn't a warning; it's the feeling of growth still in progress.

I know because I felt it too. At 39, I left emergency medicine to work for an international corporation. At 55, I built something ambitious that a board eventually decided not to support. At 57, I found myself in a classroom full of people half my age, learning alongside them, trying to figure out what comes next.

What came next was this. You don't have to rush it.

Direction matters more than speed.

Go make your moves.

ACKNOWLEDGMENTS

Writing a book may look like a solo act, but this one was built through conversation, encouragement, challenge, and generosity.

Marketing2aT exists because many people were willing to share what they've learned the hard way. They opened their calendars, told stories, offered advice, challenged my assumptions, and helped me better understand what early-career marketers need to thrive.

To the interviewees

First, thank you to the more than 130 business leaders, marketers, founders, executives, educators, consultants, and practitioners who contributed their time and wisdom to this project.

With gratitude for Liza Adams, Janelle Amos, John Arms, Barb Agoglia, Beth Bauer, George Benaroya, Vladimir Blagojević, Melanie Borden, Dawn Marie Bornheimer, Robin Bowling, Deirdre Breakenridge, Heather Brown, Mike Campbell, Angela Carrasco, Liane Caruso, Melissa Chong, John Cordier, Michelle Curran, Dan Deffit, Mariya Delano, Bill Dubiel, Lisa Fahoury, Sandy Feriz, Phyllis Ferrell, Nancy Fox, Archita Fritz, James Furbush, Annie Furlong, Debbie Gainsford, Rebecca Geier, Jakki Glivicky Geiger, Michael Gemmati, Gaspere Geraci, MD, Andre Gomez, Bahriye Goren-Gulek, Martin Greif, Ayse Guvencer, Bob Hanson, Nancy Harhut, Aaron Hassen, Toni Haugh, Tim Hillison, Jessica Holland, Scott Hurst, Kelle Johnson, Nitin Kartik, Greg Kaye, Josh King, Reid Kiser, Marina Kogan, Alex Kotler, Liz Krider, Alexandra Lazarenko, Harvey Lee, Michael Lopez, Micah Lucas, Staci Lynn, Mary MacCarthy, Sean Malony, Jessica Mekkes, Kathryn Metcalfe, Jonathan Metrick, Christian Milaster, Bob Moesta, John Munsell, Greg Nagy, Shawn Nason, Daniel Nestle, Michael Newman, Janice Nissen, Kaitlyn O'Connor, Christina O'Leary, John O'Malley, Jason Padgett, Steve Patti, Angela Paules, Kristin Perry, Caroline Petersen, Sonja Price, Brent Roberts, Geoffrey Roche, John Russo, Katie Sandoe, Mark Schaefer, Bruce Scheer, Brooke Sellas, Kenneth Simon, John Skroly, Mike Slusarz, Scott Smith, Rhonda Soest, Mark Somnolet, Kevin Spellman, David Stark, Kellie Stecher, Robin Storey, Todd Stout, Court Stroud, Andrew Sweet, David Sylvan, Courtney Todd, Melissa

Yurner, Sangram Vajre, Maebellyne Ventura, Jillian Vorce, Tim Wackel, Chris Walker, Bridgette Walshe, Andy Weiss, Zeev Wexler, Garry Wicka, Bradd Williams, Stephen Zakur, Andrei Zinkevich.

You gave this book its depth. Your stories helped me see the gap between what young marketers are taught and what employers actually expect. You spoke honestly about credibility, judgment, communication, business acumen, collaboration, curiosity, and the human side of work.

Some contributors asked not to be recognized by name, and I want to honor that trust. Thank you for speaking candidly, sharing hard-earned lessons, and helping me see the realities young marketers need to understand. Your names may not appear here, but your wisdom is woven into this book.

To my New York University School of Professional Studies faculty, academic mentors, and colleagues

Thank you to the NYU faculty, academic mentors, and staff who helped shape and sharpen my thinking as a business leader, including Albert Rizzo, Esq., Adam Braff, JD, Marc Beckman, George Benaroya, Marcela Berland, Sonjaya Singh Gaur, Ph.D., Bahriye Goren-Gulek, Martin Ihrig, Ph.D., Angie Kamath, Tariq Khan, Kathryn Landis, Bolong Li, Kathryn Metcalfe, Jose Mendoza, DBA, John O'Malley, Kathleen Rennie, Ph.D., David Rothenberg, Bart Sichel, Marc Somnolet, Court Stroud, and Joanne Tombrakos.

The work I did in graduate school gave me a stronger foundation for this book. It helped me connect marketing, strategic communication, business thinking, and professional development in a more disciplined way.

To my Yeshiva University colleagues and students

To my teaching colleagues at Yeshiva University, Katz School of Science and Health, including Christian Baldia, Heny Gabay, Joseph Panzarella, Shimon Perry, Kent Scholla, and Erek Wennerod, thank you for the conversations about what works in higher education and for the opportunity to keep practicing our craft.

To my students, it has been my privilege to play a small role in your career journey. Many of the ideas in this book became clearer because I had to explain them to real learners entering a changing profession.

To the creative team

To the designers and staff at Gallery Design Studio, including Caroline Petersen, Zoe Mazlin, Mindy Schaper, and Lacy McAdoo, thank you for helping bring the characters and visual world of this book to life.

To the early readers, reviewers, editors, designers, and advisors

Thank you to the early readers, reviewers, editors, designers, and advisors who helped improve this book. You helped sharpen the message, simplify the structure, and make the book more useful for the reader.

Special thanks to my wife, Kathryn, for her editorial expertise during countless revisions, especially the ones where you said, "This section doesn't say anything," and were loving enough to stay with me through my predictable author reactions.

INDEX

www.ingramcontent.com/pod-product-compliance
Lightning Source LLC
LaVergne TN
LVHW022051200926
848481LV00003B/864